CW00361972

UNPLANNED PREGNANCY

Debby Klein was born in Birkenhead in 1958 and gradu-
ated from University College London in 1979. She has
worked as a pregnancy counsellor for five years and
currently does freelance training and counselling in donor
insemination, sexuality, women's health issues and HIV
and AIDS. She also works in the theatre as a cabaret
performer and playwright.

Tara Kaufmann is a freelance writer and PR consultant who
has worked for numerous charities including the
Pregnancy Advisory Service and the British Pregnancy
Advisory Service. She currently works at the Royal College
of Midwives and is vice-chair of the Abortion Law Reform
Association.

UNPLANNED

PREGNANCY

MAKING THE
RIGHT CHOICE
FOR YOU

DEBBY KLEIN & TARA KAUFMANN

Foreword by Angela Willans

Thorsons
An Imprint of HarperCollinsPublishers

Thorsons
An Imprint of HarperCollins *Publishers*
77–85 Fulham Palace Road,
Hammersmith, London W6 8JB
1160 Battery Street,
San Francisco, California 94111–1213

First published by Penguin 1992
This edition published by Thorsons 1996
1 3 5 7 9 10 8 6 4 2

© Debby Klein and Tara Kaufmann 1992
Foreword © Angela Willans 1992

Debby Klein and Tara Kaufmann assert the moral
right to be identified as the authors of this work

A catalogue record for this book
is available from the British Library

ISBN 0 7225 3256 3

Printed in Great Britain
by HarperCollinsManufacturing Glasgow

All rights reserved. No part of this publication may be
reproduced, stored in a retrieval system, or transmitted,
in any form or by any means, electronic, mechanical,
photocopying, recording or otherwise, without the prior
permission of the publishers.

CONTENTS

—

FOREWORD

———

During the twenty-eight years that I've been the agony aunt on *Woman's Own*, the problem that's caused the most panic and anxiety for the people who write for help is the unplanned pregnancy. It's also the problem that gives rise to the most muddled and judgemental attitudes on the part of some politicians and moralists.

In their terms, the problem is all about the statistics on abortion, the cost to the state of single parents, and the alleged failure of schools and parents to instil 'traditional' values in the younger generation. In the terms, however, of this warm-hearted book and of the cries for help that come to me, the problem is the individual girl or woman who's thrown into despair by one small but oh-so-important biological event – the non-appearance of her period on the expected date.

Who are they, these women who long for a return to their menstrual cycle – perhaps as desperately as the sub-fertile long for the cycle to be interrupted? They're teenagers at school or college, in training, in their first jobs or with no realistic hope of employment at all; young girls living with boyfriends or on the run from home; older girls on the first steps of a career; mature single women, married women, divorced women and co-habiting women.

They may be ignorant of contraceptive methods, they may believe 'it won't happen to me', and the menopausal ones may have thought they weren't fertile any more. For many, it's a genuine accident or rationalized into one – 'the condom split', 'the Pill didn't work'. Or it was a con – 'he said he'd withdraw', 'he said he couldn't be a father', 'he promised to marry me if anything went wrong...' And, finally some of them have a subconscious longing for a baby which overrides their conscious desire to guard against conception.

What all these girls and women are *not* doing is wilfully playing Russian roulette with their reproductive systems. Neither are they consciously using abortion as a form of contraception or self-indulgently 'treating' themselves to an unwanted pregnancy. (Some anti-abortionists seem to think that we'd all want an annual abortion if there weren't someone in authority to say 'oh no you don't'.)

What every one of them needed, before they became pregnant, was straightforward education on the facts and feelings of life, love, relationships and parenthood, easy access to free contraceptive services, and personal counselling help for any difficulties or fears they encounter in these areas.

This is precisely what most young people are not getting. In its 1991 report, the Working Party on Unplanned Pregnancy, set up by the Royal College of Obstetricians and Gynaecologists, called for an end to 'the confused, complex and contradictory attitudes to sex education' in this country. This, the Working Party found, was the key factor in the low rate of contraceptive use and the high rate of abortions.

When an unplanned pregnancy is confirmed, the need is still there for information, speedy non-judgemental advice and counselling help. The overwhelming feelings expressed in the letters from the pregnant-but-don't-want-to-be are, firstly, sheer disbelief that anything so unwelcome and disruptive could have happened, and, secondly, the loneliness of a secret worry.

This book is an answer to that disbelief and loneliness. On the practical side, starting with the details of getting a pregnancy test, it offers all the information needed to choose between termination, adoption and motherhood. There are step-by-step guides to help available and the procedures for each of these options.

On the emotional side, the authors are clearly in touch with the pain inherent in the very making of these choices. They deal sensitively with doubts and uncertainties and with the feelings of guilt, regret or sadness which may be experienced when the choice has been made.

However, I don't want to give the impression that this book is all about abortion. It isn't. It's admirably evenhanded in its discussion of the options. It is neither for abortion nor against it, but for every woman's right to her own chosen, legal remedy for an unplanned pregnancy.

At present, however, it's not the law which restricts the availability of abortion, nor even the increasingly aggressive campaigning of the anti-abortion faction. The evidence of the Brook Advisory Centres' regular researches and of a comprehensive survey by the Pro-Choice Alliance is that the main stumbling-block is the inadequacy of NHS termination services. Two-thirds of the district health authorities in England and Wales are not reaching the target performance of 75 per cent of local abortions; in half the authorities the service is inadequate because of factors like outright refusal or the postponement of termination until it's too late or even dangerous.

In the face of these difficulties, you'd think that the number of abortions was decreasing. But that's to overlook the fact that every individual woman who wants an abortion is going to do all she can to get one. When you've decided, with a good deal of thought and help, that this is the only answer for you, you're not, at the first hurdle, going to believe that there's some alternative that would suit you just as well – and give up.

As a result, 52 per cent of the women having abortions in England and Wales in 1990 had to turn to the charity and private sector for them – paying between £200 and £500. Overall, on the NHS and privately, the number of abortions is rising and so is the abortion rate per thousand women of childbearing age. In 1990, there were 173,900 legal abortions performed and the figures for the year to the end of March 1991 showed an increase of 2,938 on the corresponding period the year before. The abortion rate for 1990 was 13.6, a very slight rise on the rate for the previous year.

All the workers in the field agree that a more open, broadly based approach to sex education would help to reduce these figures – so also would better support and funding for confidential contraceptive services, especially those designed for the young and unattached. In the absence of government initiatives in these two directions, all anyone can do who's associated at any level with the problem of unplanned pregnancy is to help the pregnant girl or woman arrive as soon as possible at a remedy that suits her and her circumstances.

Tara Kaufmann and Debby Klein meet that need very well indeed – this is a realistic, compassionate book in the true counselling tradition.

Angela Willans

ACKNOWLEDGEMENTS

We would like to thank the following for their help and advice:

Toni Belfield (FPA); Melissa Benn; Jenny Benwell; Paul Lincoln (NFCA); Peter Molyneux; Tony Parsons (Senior Lecturer in Obstetrics & Gynaecology, Warwick University); Terry Patterson; Positively Women; Kath Pringle; Jane Roe (Pro-Choice Alliance); Karen Talbot; Pat Thompson (Womens Health); Lesley Thomson.

Thanks also to Celia Robinson and Sarah McNair for help with the typing.

INTRODUCTION

———

Unplanned pregnancy can be one of the most difficult and distressing experiences a women has to face. It is a much more common experience than many people realize: nearly one in three births are unplanned, while one in three women can expect to have an abortion in her lifetime.

Unplanned pregnancies are not a new phenomenon: previous generations of women were expected to bear and raise children that were not planned or even necessarily wanted. These days, increased personal freedoms, work opportunities and availability of birth control have allowed women more choice over their childbearing, and more control over their lives.

The availability of contraception leads many people to wonder why unplanned pregnancy happens at all – and this attitude is reflected in the guilt and shame felt by many of those women for whom this book is written. It is easy to forget that we all take risks and make mistakes in this area of human affairs, as much as in any other; and that the chance of becoming pregnant from any one act of unprotected sex is around 20%.

Even where a woman is using contraception, she can become pregnant. All forms of birth control have some failure rate: a recent survey showed that over 70% of unplanned pregnancies had been conceived while using contraception. In America, research has suggested that about 6% of pill users, and 16% of condom users, will have an unplanned pregnancy in the course of one year.

There are many other reasons why women get pregnant. They may not use contraception because they don't know how or where to get it, or because they don't know how to use it effectively. They may think they are infertile, or menopausal, or maybe their partner will not let them protect themselves adequately. For some women there may be a subconscious desire to test their fertility or femininity, or the strength of a particular relationship. It can also be a way of crying for help: a signal of despair, anger or loneliness.

Although we use the term 'unplanned pregnancy' throughout this book, it is also intended for women whose pregnancies were planned yet have become problematic. This may be because of an unforeseen change of circumstances – redundancy, homelessness or divorce – or because of medical problems or foetal abnormality.

There are many myths and stereotypes about unplanned pregnancy: most of them cruel and inaccurate. It is often assumed that single women will want to terminate unplanned pregnancies, and that married women will not; that Catholic women will not have abortion, and that black women will choose single parenthood; that abortion is commonly used as a form of birth control, and that it is more difficult, more dangerous, and more reprehensible than continuing an unplanned pregnancy.

From our combined experience of many years of working in pregnancy advisory services, we can vouch that unplanned pregnancy affects women of all cultures, classes and religious backgrounds. We also know, both from counselling and personal experience, that each woman's emotional reaction to unplanned pregnancy is varied and individual and cannot be predicted in advance.

We have tried to reflect the diversity of women's experience in the following pages. Much of the first three chapters is concerned with the decision-making process: for some readers this may be superfluous, as they will already be clear about what course of action is best for them, and only need the information that is included to help them translate that conviction into action. Other readers may find their decision more difficult and painful, and will find this book most effective as a supplement to individual counselling.

For some readers it may be important to know where this book 'stands' on abortion. We both wholeheartedly support every woman's right to choose to terminate a problem pregnancy, but that does not mean we believe that abortion is always the right choice for every woman. Many loved and wanted children started as unplanned pregnancies, after all, and for many women unplanned pregnancy provides the catalyst to their first serious consideration of the place of motherhood in their lives. The crucial point is that there are no 'right' or 'wrong' answers to unplanned pregnancy: the only acceptable solution is one that is chosen by the woman herself and based on her individual circumstances.

So, this book does not provide any 'answers' – no book, no counsellor, no friend ever can. The only 'answer' you can find to unplanned pregnancy is within yourself and it is our aim to give the information and guidance needed to help find that answer. There are no guarantees that the choice you make will be the 'right' one, or that you will not have moments of regret in the years to come. With sufficient information, self-awareness and sympathetic support, however, you should be able to come to terms and learn to live with the decision you must make. Whatever you choose, we hope you will find that the rewards will outweigh the drawbacks, and that you can move forward with a positive respect and trust for yourself and for the decision you have reached.

CHAPTER ONE

A POSITIVE RESULT?

___

This could be the first time you've had to face unplanned pregnancy, or you may have been in this situation before. Maybe you're someone who worries every time your period is late, or perhaps you just never thought this could happen to you . . . Many women, when they first realize they might be pregnant, wonder 'Why me?'

There are many myths around unwanted pregnancy: one is that it only happens to careless women. As we have said, no method of birth control is infallible, and there are also many valid reasons why women don't use it or have problems with it. Still, you might be feeling guilty or foolish if you took a risk or if sex was unplanned. Alternatively, if you have been using contraception, then this pregnancy may seem horribly unfair.

If you have taken a risk, try not to be too hard on yourself. We all take risks every day of our lives – that's part of being human and it doesn't mean we are irresponsible or stupid. Sex itself is a risky business. It is also an area of our lives which is deeply personal and complex and where it is not always easy to be sensible and in control. If you didn't use birth control on this occasion, remember all the times when you did use it – one slip-up doesn't wipe out all those years of being careful. If you made a conscious choice to stop using contraception, then remind yourself of the reasons why. Maybe the pill made you feel unwell, or your partner wasn't co-operative, or there was part of you that did want to get pregnant. If you got pregnant the first time you had sex or at the beginning of a new relationship you may be feeling particularly distressed and cheated at how the excitement of this new experience can be lost in the worry about what to do next.

ARE YOU REALLY PREGNANT?

If you think you may be pregnant, then it is important that you take action as soon as possible – **don't** wait until your second period is overdue, and **don't** hope that by ignoring the problem you will make it go away.

You may be alerted to a possible problem by the following, which are all common symptoms of pregnancy:

- **missed period**
- **tender, swollen breasts**
- **darkening nipples**
- **needing to pee more frequently**
- **feeling tired and drained**
- **nausea and/or vomiting**
- **food cravings**
- **sensitivity to cigarette smoke**
- **increased vaginal discharge**
- **constipation**

None of these symptoms mean you are definitely pregnant. All of them can be due to other causes, such as stress or illness. Likewise, you may not have any symptoms, yet still be pregnant. It is even possible to have light periods **while** pregnant, so be aware of any changes in your body, but don't altogether rely on them.

The best way to confirm a pregnancy is to have a pregnancy test done. The most common form is a urine test which measures the level of Human Chorionic Gonadotrophin (HCG) in your urine. This can be used as early as the first day of your expected period, and as late as the sixteenth week of pregnancy. There are also older forms of urine test which are only effective when your period is fourteen days overdue. Pregnancy can also be confirmed with a blood test or internal examination.

A note on emergency contraception

If you have had unprotected sex within the past five days, you can still stop pregnancy occurring by using emergency birth control – also known as 'postcoital contraception' or the 'morning-after pill'.

There are two types of emergency contraception:

1 Hormonal pills taken within 72 hours
2 IUD insertion within five days
(The IUD can be left in as your regular form of birth control, if you wish.)

You can get emergency contraception from:

- **Family Planning Clinics**
- **BPAS, Marie Stopes and other pregnancy advisory clinics**
- **Brook Advisory Centres**
- **some GPs**

This cannot replace regular birth control, but it is a very good emergency measure (see Help and Information, p. 174).

WHERE TO GET A TEST

There are a number of places where you can get a pregnancy test: your choice will depend on local availability, cost, your need for privacy and follow-up help and information.

Your GP may do a pregnancy test free of charge. Unfortunately, many GPs will need to send your urine sample to a hospital laboratory, and it may take up to two weeks for you to get the result back.

Family Planning Clinics will usually do an immediate test free of charge, but some restrict this service to women who are already registered with them.

Brook Advisory Clinics offer free tests to young women: counselling and practical help are also available.

BPAS and Marie Stopes Clinics offer immediate pregnancy testing from about £7, and specialist help and counselling as required. BPAS also provide a postal testing service: be sure to parcel your sample securely and to include your name and address.

Home tests, available from chemists, cost around £8–£10. They are very reliable these days, and show a result between 5 and 30 minutes. You do need to follow the instructions very carefully, and it may be a drawback not to have professional advice immediately to hand. However, the privacy of this method may be important to you.

Pharmacists sometimes do their own testing service. Result time and cost varies, and there is no follow-up help available.

Women's Centres sometimes offer pregnancy testing for a small fee. Your local CAB should have details of the address and opening hours.

Commercial pregnancy testing services are located in most big cities, and can be found in phone directories under 'Pregnancy Testing'.

LIFE and some other anti-abortion organizations offer pregnancy testing and advice, often free of charge. They will not help you to arrange abortion.

Many of these places will ask you to bring in a urine sample. It is best to use your first pee of the morning, carried in a clean, labelled bottle with a tight screw-on cap. A small jar or pill bottle will do, providing you have cleaned and rinsed it thoroughly. You will also need to tell the pregnancy tester the date of your last period, and the name of any drugs (including contraception) you are taking.

A false positive pregnancy test is very rare, but it is possible to get a false negative result, especially very early in pregnancy. It is, therefore, a good idea to have another test a week later. A doctor will be able to confirm pregnancy through internal examination from about four weeks' gestation. This is done by inserting a speculum, which hold apart the walls of your vagina. S/he then puts the fingers of one hand in your vagina, and the other hand on your stomach, so as to feel the size of your womb. This is not very comfortable, but shouldn't hurt. You can make it easier for yourself by relaxing: try tightening your muscles as if to stop yourself peeing, and then pushing your pelvic muscles gently downwards while breathing out.

If you are aged 16 or over, doctors have to treat you in confidence – they cannot tell your parents or anyone else about why you are seeing them, and you do not need parental permission for any medical treatment.

If you are under 16, the doctor will try very hard to get you to involve your parents, as parents' permission is usually needed to give you any medical treatment such as an abortion. If you refuse to tell them, s/he will have to decide whether you are mature enough not to need parental consent. The doctor may say s/he won't help you unless you do involve your parents, but wouldn't usually tell your parents without your permission. The legal position over this is unclear, however, and it is only fair to warn you that we can't guarantee your doctor **won't** tell your parents if you are pregnant. If you are worried about this, go to a Brook Clinic or one of the charitable pregnancy advisory services, who will be sympathetic. Even they might not be able to give you medical treatment without your parents' involvement, but they will not tell your parents – or your doctor – without your permission.

DEALING WITH IMMEDIATE FEELINGS

Even if you have begun to consider how you might feel if the test is positive, you could still experience an initial shock when you get the results. This may only last a few hours, but for some women it can go on for days and even weeks. It is at this point that you are confronted with having to make a decision. You could also find that, however hard you try to act and think normally, there is a persistent sense of unreality about the whole situation. Because unplanned pregnancy is still regarded as a rare and terrible event by many people it can seem absurd that this is happening to you and not to someone else. It may seem like an appalling piece of bad luck that you don't deserve, a personal failure or even a punishment for bad behaviour.

The first step is simply to allow yourself to experience whatever unfamiliar or contradictory emotions come bubbling to the surface. There is no right way to feel about an unwanted pregnancy. Your reactions will be unique and will depend on what else is going on in your life, your feelings about yourself and your relationships, and how you usually respond to crises.

You may feel angry, powerless, distressed or panicky. You didn't choose to be pregnant; it could be a struggle to regain a sense of control. Some women have a strong sense of their bodies being 'invaded' and the physical symptoms of pregnancy are painful reminders of their inability to make the whole thing just 'go away'.

It is possible that you will feel calm and relatively unemotional. Some women are apologetic about this, imagining other people will see them as callous or peculiar if they are not sufficiently anguished. There is no law which says unplanned pregnancy has to be a devastating experience. If you are clear about what you want and confident of your ability to cope then your decision may be perfectly straightforward.

It is also possible that you will feel excited and happy to find that you are pregnant. You could be thrilled by your ability to conceive and fascinated by the changes in your body. This is as true for women who choose abortions as for those who continue with the pregnancy. The experience of being pregnant and the possibilities of motherhood can give you valuable information about what you want from the future even if you decide the time is not yet right to have a child.

Because unplanned pregnancy presents you with a practical

problem that you must 'sort out', to have to confront painful emotions at the same time can be daunting, especially if your feelings seem outside your control. It may be tempting to clamp down on them and concentrate on the practical aspects of your decision. In the end, it is entirely up to you how much you question and explore your feelings about the choice you make, but it is possible to express how you feel without being overwhelmed by it.

Your first reactions to your pregnancy are important; if you can, give yourself some space to let them sink in. Try to organize a few hours away from the demands of work, children or other commitments. Cancel social arrangements unless they are with people who can support you. Decide whether you want to be on your own or with someone you're close to and then just let yourself do what comes naturally, whether it's having a good cry, a tantrum or sitting quietly feeling numb. Concentrate on putting your own needs first for a while. It may be doubly hard to ask for what you want at the moment if you are feeling particularly vulnerable or angry with yourself.

What do you need right now? It could be an evening with a close friend, a few drinks and a large box of tissues; your partner giving you their undivided attention and lots of hugs; or being left alone to have a good scream and throw pillows at the wall. Try at least to be somewhere for a while where you don't have to pretend you're fine and nothing's happened.

Although you may need to act quickly that doesn't mean you have to rush into a decision while you're still in a panic. Allowing yourself a short breathing space can actually save you time in the long run, because you will feel less vulnerable and a little clearer about what you want and what information and help you need.

Your feelings will also be affected by the circumstances in which you got pregnant. If you are married or in a steady relationship, you might be relieved that you don't have to make the decision alone but it is a situation which will test the strength of your relationship; that in itself can be unnerving. If you are split-ting up with your partner, then the pregnancy will be bound up with your attitude to ending the relationship. If your partner is leaving you or has been particularly hurtful, then it might take you some time to disentangle the anger, lust for revenge or grief in order to make the right decision for your future.

If you are having a sexual relationship that you feel guilty about, or one that you think society, or your family or the church would disapprove of, then this can compound your distress. You may feel that the pregnancy is in some way a punishment for having sex rather than simply an accident. We are all guilty of making moral judgements about other people's lifestyles, even if we try to be tolerant and accepting of difference. There is a huge amount of collective judgement and disapproval out in the world. Sometimes it is hard to ignore this and to continue to have confi-dence in the choices we make in our lives; it is also possible to internalize this so that we join ranks with those who are critical and end up seeing ourselves as bad or worthless.

Even nowadays, when there is much more choice around lifestyles and sexual relationships, women are still given a lot of mixed messages about how they should behave. On the one hand we are all supposed to be sexually liberated and on the other, women are still called 'slags' if they have more than one sexual partner. Phrases like 'being promiscuous', 'sleeping around' and 'she's anybody's' are not designed to make us feel good about ourselves. This can make you feel vulnerable if the pregnancy is the result of a one-night stand or a brief affair. If you are confident about yourself and your lifestyle then it is easier to shrug off the negative stereotypes. Even if the one-night stand was a disaster or the affair a big mistake you can accept that it's no reflection on you as a person. However, if you feel bad about yourself, you could end up feeling guilty or humiliated.

Sex is also a private thing between two people, whereas unplanned pregnancy usually means you have to involve others, including complete strangers, whether you decide to have an abor-tion or to have the baby. This in itself can cause a lot of anxiety if you are concerned about other people making judgements about you. It is a justifiable fear but you could also find that those whom you tell are accepting and supportive. After all, it is a situation that millions of women throughout the world are familiar with; many of them would understand how you feel. Pause and imagine for a minute what it would be like if men got pregnant. They'd probably expect total support and understanding, free abortion on demand, a salary and a halo if they continued the pregnancy. You may have to wait a few hundred years for the last three but the first two are no less than you deserve.

WHO TO TELL

We will look more closely at deciding who to tell in the next chapter, but it is important to think from the start about who you trust and what support you can offer. Once you have told someone you can't 'untell' them; you need to be sure they will respect your confidentiality and won't tell anyone else without your permission.

Ideally, the first person you tell should be someone who will listen to and accept how you feel rather than overwhelm you with their own feelings or heavy-handed advice. If you are in a relationship, then your partner may seem the obvious person to turn to. Your partner may be extremely supportive but if you aren't getting on, or if you suspect your partner will pressurize you into a decision, then consider talking to a close friend or counsellor first.

You may be lucky and surrounded by close friends and family. Sometimes friends, and particularly women friends, are the ones who are able to give support without having too much invested in your decision. It is harder for your family to be as objective as your friends, but, if you are close to them, it could seem perfectly natural to turn to them first.

However, it is not always so easy to get the support you need. You could feel that your family and even your friends will disapprove of you and react unsympathetically. You may not have close friends that you trust or you could be living far away from them. If you are feeling alone or unsure how people in your life will react then it can be a good idea to talk to a counsellor. Counselling should be confidential and the counsellor can help you make decisions or simply support the decisions you've already made. A good counsellor won't make moral judgements about you or be shocked by your feelings or your situation. The added advantage is that a counsellor is completely outside your life, so whatever you say will have no repercussions on you or your relationships at a later date.

You could also talk to your GP but this is probably only a good idea if you already have a good relationship with them or if you think they will be supportive.

Remember, if you are very distressed or isolated you can always phone the Samaritans. You don't have to feel suicidal or at the end of your tether to ring them; they are there as a 'sympathetic ear' for anyone who may have no one else to turn to at that particular time. The Samaritans run a twenty-four hour phone line so you can call them at any time. It also may feel safe using the telephone as the other person doesn't know who you are and you can end the call whenever you want.

OPTIONS

It would be nice if you could just turn the clock back and become unpregnant, but that is not one of the options open to you. Instead, you are faced with making a decision which may be very difficult and painful. It will certainly be irreversible, and will affect many areas of your life: your relationships, your career and your future.

The following chapters give you three main options, plus the information you need to reach the choice that is best for you.

Chapter Five tells you about abortion. Providing you have legal grounds under the 1967 Act, and can find a sympathetic doctor, you could choose to terminate your pregnancy.

Chapter Seven is about motherhood: continuing your pregnancy and bringing up your baby by yourself or with a partner.

Chapter Eight is concerned with adoption and fostering, which means you continue the pregnancy, but then give your child to another family to care for either temporarily (fostering) or permanently (adoption).

None of these choices are 'good' or 'bad'. They all have advantages and drawbacks, and only you can decide which will be best for your situation. But there is help available to aid you in making that decision, and to support you through it.

CHAPTER TWO

MAKING YOUR DECISION

———

Making a decision about an unplanned pregnancy does not have to be difficult. You may know right from the beginning what you want to do. Sometimes there is a clear voice saying 'Right, I want an abortion. How do I get one?' or 'This may not easy, but I know I want this baby.' Fewer women choose adoption and fostering, but these could also be positive choices. All the options will be discussed in more detail in later chapters.

However, making this decision can also be quite a complex process and bring in its wake contradictory emotions and unexpected feelings. Even if you are clear about what you want you could worry whether you are doing the right thing, feel guilty or frightened of the consequences, or you may be genuinely undecided about which option is best.

Taking responsibility for your decision can put you in a lonely and frightening position. It is natural to be irritated with a partner who says, 'It's entirely up to you,' or a counsellor who insists that they can't make up your mind for you. Sometimes it is tempting to avoid responsibility and allow someone else to influence your decision, or to drift into an abortion or a pregnancy that you are not sure you want. But it is much harder to come to terms with a situation when it is too late to change it. Taking control now means it is less likely that you will feel trapped or powerless later on; however frustrating or painful the process is, it can be reassuring to know that you are in charge of your life.

TAKING TIME

One of the obvious factors in choosing whether to have an abortion or continue a pregnancy is the time limit. It may take you several years to decide whether you want a divorce or a new job, but this is a choice you have to make in a matter of weeks, or sometimes days.

The first thing you need to know is how many weeks' pregnant you are. It can be difficult to remember exactly when your last period was so don't rely entirely on dates. Some women continue to have period-type bleeding after they conceive. A doctor should be able to give you a fairly accurate estimation through an internal examination but, if the doctor is vague or you disagree, get a second opinion. Obviously, the earlier in the pregnancy you are, the more time you have to think things through, but at any stage it is possible to feel that you are racing against the biological clock. You cannot ignore the time factor, but try not to let it panic you.

It would be great if whenever we had an important decision to make our other responsibilities would just melt away and we had all the peace and time we needed, preferably with someone to cook our meals and attend to our every whim. In the real world it may not be possible to take unlimited time off work or away from childcare and other commitments. However, you should try to put yourself first as much as you can.

- **It is the quality rather than the quantity of time that is important.** Plan an afternoon or an evening (or more) when you can focus on your decision and how you feel about it. Ideally you need to be somewhere where you feel relaxed and won't be interrupted.
- **Try to cut down on other commitments.** Decide how much time you can take off work or whether someone else can look after the children. Cancel the visit to the dentist or dinner with your parents. Don't feel bad about telling a white lie. If you had the flu you wouldn't be able to carry on as normal, so why should you at the moment?

- **You may dread sitting down and really thinking about what to do.** It might seem a lot easier to keep busy and put off making a decision for as long as possible. Sometimes deciding what to do involves confronting your worst fears, but unfortunately avoiding the situation won't make it go away. It takes a lot of courage to face what is painful and frightening about the choices open to you but it can be much more positive than continually running away.

- **Decide who else you want to talk to.** Whether it is your partner, family or friends, make sure that they are available when you need them.

- **You don't have to delay making practical arrangements if you are considering a termination.** If you want a termination on the NHS there may be delays anyway, so start the ball rolling by seeing your GP and arranging appointments: this doesn't commit you to going ahead with the operation. If you go to a pregnancy advisory bureau you can always make an appointment just to see a counsellor, and book the actual operation at a later date.

- **If you use this time constructively it will take away the feeling of panic.** Weighing up the options carefully does not mean that you are dithering. If you have already made your decision you might want to spend some time looking at how you can come to terms with it and feel positive about the future.

ASSESSING YOUR SITUATION

The tools that you need to make the right decision are a clear picture of your present situation, what you want for the future and good information about the different options available to you.

It is not always easy to take an objective look at what is going on in our lives. We often have high expectations of ourselves and other people; it is sometimes quite hard to sort out what we want from what is actually going on. For instance, you may be very committed to your partner and feel he would make a wonderful father, but have to face the fact that he has always said he doesn't want children and that he is unlikely to change his mind. Likewise, you may want to have a child when you are financially secure but have to acknowledge that you are up to your ears in debt or that you want to change jobs in the next few months.

Usually, we are quite perceptive about our lives if we give ourselves a chance to think clearly about them for a while. Sometimes writing things down or talking to a close friend or a counsellor will help. It may be harder to be clear about what you want from the future as there are so many different possibilities to consider. It may also be a challenge to separate what you want from what is expected of you. An unplanned pregnancy can touch on every area of your life including work, education, relationships, lifestyle, living arrangements, money and family, as well as high-lighting your hopes and dreams for your future.

You will need to consider some or all of these factors in your decision. Sometimes crises make us look afresh at things we normally take for granted. When you contemplate giving up work to have a baby, you may realize just how important and stimu-lating your job is; on the other hand, you may decide that your work is deathly dull and that being a mother seems a much more fulfilling prospect.

The decision could be harder if you are unhappy or dissatis-fied with your life at the moment. Many women find abortion an easier choice when they have positive reasons for not wanting a child at this stage of your life. If you want to travel the world; you're happy being free and single; you already have a child/chil-dren you love; you are valued at work; you and your partner have plans for the future – then these things can outweigh any loss or pain involved in terminating the pregnancy.

If you are stuck in a rut, or life is fraught with problems and diffi-culties, then it may be hard to see anything positive in having an abortion. If you feel that you aren't getting much out of life then it can be particularly painful to contemplate 'giving up' your baby. Equally, you may be aware that having a child is not going to solve the problems that already exist but is more likely to create a whole lot more. It can help to write things down when you are considering all this. Putting your thoughts and feelings on paper can help to clarify what you want as well as giving you something to refer back to when the doubts creep in. It could also help to structure your thoughts by using the exercises in this book. They may not all be appropriate to you – pick and choose which ones are useful.

EXERCISE 1
Working out your priorities

- **Write a list of the things you value in your life at the moment.** Don't think too much about it, just put down as many as you can. Include more general things – e.g., my independence – as well as specifics – e.g., having a good time with my friends.

- **Read over the list and underline the five most important.**

- **Go through the five and write down two or three reasons why each one is important.**

Example **My job**

1 I like the people I work with – I like being part of a team.
2 I know I'm good at what I do – I like being efficient.
3 I know it's unlikely I'll get made redundant – I
   appreciate having a regular wage.

- **Repeat the exercise, this time writing a list of things you want from the future.** Don't censor yourself. Be as mundane or as fanciful as you like. Pick out the most important and write down the reasons why.

- **Reread what you've written and think about the**

information it's given you. Was it a struggle to think of the positive aspects of your life, or was it easy? What about your ambitions? Are they things you can achieve in the next few years or are they far-off dreams?

Compare the two lists. Is there a big difference in what you have now and what you want, or do they tie in quite neatly? What does this tell you about yourself? Is security really important to you or do you enjoy taking risks? How confident do you feel about getting what you want? Does your future happiness rely a lot on other people?

- **Now start to consider your decision in the light of what you've written.** Imagine continuing the pregnancy. How would that affect your present life? What about your future plans?

- **Now consider a termination (and adoption if this is a viable option for you) – how would it affect your life now?** What about the future? How different would it be if you didn't have the baby? Write down a few statements about each option.

Doing this exercise may help you to decide how important having a child is in your life, and might help you to consider what you may have to change or give up in order to have a child now.

Is being a mother an important part of your future plans? If it is, how much do the circumstances matter? Do you feel strongly that you must be financially secure or is material comfort relatively unimportant? Do you only want a child in the context of a steady relationship or do you feel quite positive about being a single mother? If you cannot realistically cope with a child now, how do you feel about having a termination? If you see having children as very central to your identity, then abortion could be a painful choice. This does not mean it is the wrong choice. If you accept this, it could make it easier to decide what you really want.

If children play little or no part in your present and future plans, does this make your choice simpler or are you still unsure what to do? Perhaps you feel differently about termination now that you're actually pregnant. Maybe you feel you should have the baby because having an abortion is selfish, will displease other people or make you feel terrible afterwards. Having a child because you want one is a much easier option than having a child because you can't face having an abortion. If you do decide to continue the pregnancy, then it will be important for you to find positive reasons for doing so.

WHAT INFORMATION DO I NEED?

It is important that you have all the information that you need to make the right decision. The better informed you are the more you will be able to take control and the less you will have to go round in circles thinking 'what if . . .?' By assessing your life and expectations of the future you already have a lot of valuable information. You may need to carry on getting information from yourself; really finding out what you want and what your fears are. You will also need information from other people. How will the people close to you support you if you have a baby? How will your partner feel if you have an abortion? Finally, you will need practical information about what services and benefits are available to you.

Write a list of all the questions you want an answer to. If you are considering more than one option write two (or three) lists. Put down everything you can think of. Work out who can provide you with the answers. This book will give you details of where to get practical information. The following is an example of some of the questions that might be relevant.

Example Abortion

1 What are the medical risks of an abortion at this stage?
2 If I have a termination will I feel alright about it? Can I get counselling after it?
3 Can I get a termination on the NHS? Can I afford to go privately?
4 Will the abortion stop me having children in the future?
5 How will it affect my relationship?
6 Is it confidential? Will I have to tell my parents/my GP/the father?
7 How long will I have to wait for the operation?
8 Will it hurt?
9 If I can't get an NHS abortion, can I borrow the money?
10 Does everyone feel guilty and hate themselves afterwards?

Example Keeping the baby

1 Does my job offer maternity leave?
2 What effect will having a baby have on my promotion prospects?
3 Will having a baby be too much of a strain on my relationship?
4 Do I need financial help from other people? Can I ask my parents/partner for help?
5 Can I afford to live on benefit? What am I entitled to?
6 Can I have the baby and stay where I'm living? If I move, what are the options?
7 Can I cope being a single parent? Who can I ask for support?
8 What are the nursery/childminder facilities like in my area?
9 What will it be like to take a few years off work? Can I work part-time? Do I want to?
10 What sort of relationship do I want the baby to have with its father?
11 Will I still see my friends or am I going to be really isolated?

Obviously some of these questions are easier to answer than others. Finding out how much child benefit is these days is a lot simpler than deciding whether your relationship will last. But by addressing these questions you should get a clearer idea of who you need to talk to and what help and support is available.

TRUSTING YOURSELF TO MAKE THE RIGHT DECISION

No one is better able than you to make the right decision and you have all the skills you need to make it. It is much easier though, if you start out by being on your own side. Usually we are tougher on ourselves than we are on other people in our lives. Most of us have a critical voice inside our head and sometimes this voice can be very punishing. Women are particularly prone to self-punishment because we are encouraged from an early age to be carers, and to put other people's needs before our own.

Because problem pregnancy can bring up deep feelings about motherhood, sexuality, and control over our fertility it makes many women feel vulnerable. Abortion is not as taboo as it was some years ago, but there is still a prevalent opinion that is is, at best, a necessary evil. Similarly, having a baby when you are very young, or on your own, or when you have a large family or little money, can also be disapproved of.

It is easy to see, therefore, why some women perceive this as a no-win situation and continue to feel bad about themselves. Although unplanned pregnancy can be a painful and distressing experience, it does not mean that you have to regard yourself as a failure. If you do, then the punishing voice is likely to have a field day. It may sound something like this:

You are really so stupid. You know you shouldn't have come off the pill. You're old enough to know better and this is the worst time to get pregnant. It's hopeless. There's no way you can cope with a baby now, so you'll have to get rid of it. If you do, you'll feel terrible – you said you'd never have an abortion. Just think how ashamed your father would be if he found out. You're such a failure.

It is unlikely that we would ever let a friend speak to us like this, but we often talk to ourselves in this way. If it were a friend you could slam down the phone or walk out of the room, but you can't escape from yourself so easily.

The first thing to do, if you are giving yourself a hard time, is simply to acknowledge that it is happening. If that voice has been with you for a couple of decades, then it is not going to vanish overnight. The punishing voice could be there for different reasons. It may be that you don't feel very good about yourself and are continually setting up expectations that are impossible to meet. It could stem from the fact that you were given little encouragement or positive feedback as a child, or that your parents had ridiculously high or unhelpful expectations of you. It may be there because it's easier to be angry at yourself than somebody else. This is especially true for women. Perhaps you are frightened of repeating past mistakes or are frightened of getting it wrong. Whatever the reason, this inner voice isn't going to be much help in making your decision. If you are giving yourself a tough time try the following exercise.

EXERCISE 2
Finding the protector in yourself

- **Identify the negative, disparaging voice.** Imagine that it is someone else talking to you. What are they saying? Write down all the statements beginning with 'You are . . .' and add whatever else the voice comes out with – your shortcomings, failures, reasons why you've behaved wrongly or stupidly.
- **Have a look at what you've written.** Does it sound familiar? Where have you heard it before? Give the voice a personality. What does it look like? Does it remind you of someone you know?
- **What does it feel like being on the end of all this abuse?** What would happen if you asked the voice to shut up? Would it? Or would it carry on regardless?

24

- Is this abusive person the best person to help you make a decision? If not, then who would be? Think of the qualities you would want from someone who was giving you advice. Maybe make a list. Perhaps they need to be kind, perceptive, compassionate – someone who understands your dilemma and won't judge you harshly. If you knew someone like this what would they look like and how would they sound?
- Try and fix an image of these two characters in your mind – the punisher and the protector. Imagine that the protector is going to take control. They are going to help you make the right decision and they are going to keep the punishing voice in line.
- What sort of advice does the protective voice give you? It may be the sort of advice you would give a close friend who was in your predicament. Use the protective personality to give yourself the sort of consideration you would give to someone you really cared about. This may help you to reject the punishing voice when it comes up.

It may seem a little bizarre at first, giving names and personalities to your feelings, but it is a useful way to begin to accept and feel in control of powerful emotions rather than feeling that they are in control of you.

LOOKING AFTER YOUR FEELINGS

Of course, not all difficult emotions are punishing. You could be very sad that this isn't the ideal time to have a child and angry with your situation or the people in your life. Looking after yourself isn't about side-stepping painful emotions but about being able to express them in a way that isn't destructive.

For some women, making the decision is a painful and complex process – but this can mean that once you have made it you will feel a great sense of relief. Many women who choose termination do a lot of their grieving at this stage and find that once they have had the abortion they can come to terms with it more easily than they thought possible. Equally, women who choose to continue the pregnancy may be beset by doubts and anxieties at the outset but find more positive feelings emerge later.

It is important to remind yourself that there is no correct way to feel about your pregnancy. Neither should you assume that you are callous or unnatural if a termination appears to be straightforward. Many women from a variety of backgrounds see abortion as an obvious solution to a practical problem – it can be a positive choice if you feel confident of your right to control your own fertility.

HEAD VERSUS HEART

Some women believe that if they pay too much attention to their feelings this could actually prevent them from making the right decision. Others talk of the split between the emotional and the practical – in other words, their head wanting one thing and their heart another. For instance, you may be thrilled to be pregnant and long to go ahead but know there are problems about finances and accommodation. Or you may be in an ideal situation to have the baby you always thought you wanted but just feel instinctively that the timing of the pregnancy isn't right.

Try to listen to both your head and your heart. You need to be able to acknowledge what you really want as well as being realistic about the practical difficulties. If you are going round in a circle try the following exercise.

EXERCISE 3
Fantasy and practicality

- **Take some time alone, somewhere you feel relaxed.** Forget about the practical considerations and anxieties for a while. Let your heart speak first. Allow yourself to build a fantasy of what the ideal option would be.
- **Write the details of your fantasy down if it helps you to remember them.** If your fantasy is about continuing the pregnancy, build up as detailed a picture as you can. What are all the positive things about being a mother? How do you see yourself and the child in one year's time? What about five years or ten years on? Forget about the dirty nappies and the money worries – just think about the good bits. Note how you feel as you do this. Is it excited? Sad? Nervous?
- **If your fantasy is about the pregnancy just disappearing, allow yourself to develop this.** What would it be like to have a guilt-free abortion? What freedoms would you gain? Imagine your life over the next year and imagine all the things you enjoy doing. Note how you feel.
- **Allow yourself to enjoy the fantasy you've created.** This is what you would want in an ideal world. Now let the practical/head voice speak. Let this voice question the fantasy you've created. Don't let the practical side of you destroy the fantasy – just question it.
- **Your practical side will be interested in how you're going to survive in the real world.** Now you have an idea of what you really want let your practical side help you work out whether it is achievable. By letting the two sides have a constructive debate, you will be able to build a picture that is neither totally bleak nor simply pie in the sky. Notice the questions that keep coming up – you may have listed them earlier – are you now able to provide answers? When you put your fantasy under scrutiny does it melt away or are you able to see ways around the obstacles?

Although your doubts and worries won't vanish overnight you may have a better idea by now which option is best for you. If you are still finding it impossible to make a firm decision have a look at the section on ambivalence in Chapter Three, 'Conflict with Yourself and with Others'. Also consider talking things through with a counsellor.

CONFRONTING YOUR FEARS

It is possible to make a decision but to be fearful of the consequences. You haven't got a crystal ball, you can't look into the future and reassure yourself that everything's going to be fine, and that is scary. However, turning round and confronting your fears can in itself be quite liberating.

Some women are very frightened about having an abortion. They may believe that they will never be the same again, that they won't be able to have children in the future or even that they will never wake up from the anaesthetic. These fears don't have a logical basis but that doesn't mean they are easy to dismiss. It doesn't matter whether your fears are dramatic or relatively minor, you should pay attention to them. If you examine your fear it can give you some idea where it comes from. It may be that it stems from feeling out of control, or from a belief that you are going to be punished for making this decision. Getting good information and talking with a counsellor or with medical staff can help to reassure you. If you are worried about your reactions after the abortion, make sure that at this stage you will have access to good support.

You could be equally frightened by the thought of continuing the pregnancy. You may worry that you won't make a good mother, that you won't be able to make ends meet, that you will resent your child. Again, you will need to confront your fear in order to work out what you need from the future – and also to decide whether your worries are realistic. Remember, there is no such thing as the ideal mother. In order to cope you should pay attention to your own needs as well as your child's.

Making the decision about your pregnancy can give you valuable insight into what you want from your life, your feelings about having children, and under what circumstances you would choose to be a mother (if at all). It may be a frustrating or upsetting experience but it doesn't have to be a negative one.

Remember

- Take time to assess your situation and the different options.
- Make sure you have all the information you need.
- Don't punish yourself for being in this situation.
- Believe in your ability to make the right decision.
- Look after yourself. Your emotional well-being is a priority.

WHO SHOULD I TELL?

There are a number of people whom you may need or want to talk to about your pregnancy. They might include your partner, friends, family, GP and other health professionals or counsellors. You could feel some people (the father, for instance) have a right to know or you may want to share the responsibility for making the decision. If you want a termination, you will need to tell your GP or to talk to a private or charity agency. You may tell people because you want advice or support or even revenge. If you are considering continuing the pregnancy, you may want to sound out the reactions of your family and friends, perhaps to know what help is available. You might need to find out if you can carry on living at home or if your job will still be there for you; you may need to involve social services.

If you are lucky, the people you tell will be sympathetic and helpful and will support your right to make your own decision.

Sadly, this is not going to be everyone's experience. The people around you may react strongly, and sometimes negatively, to your pregnancy. If they do, this can put you in a difficult position at a time when you are already feeling distressed.

It is useful to consider carefully who you are going to tell, what you need from them, and what the likelihood is of you getting it. The people you're close to may be very caring and give you a lot of support but they could also be shocked, angry or extremely upset. You could end up bearing the brunt of this or at least feeling you have to look after them as well as yourself.

Keeping the pregnancy secret can also be a strain. You might have to act being cheerful and energetic when you feel anything but, and live in terror that someone's eagle eye will spot the frequent trips to the toilet or the early morning nausea.

Who in your life is best able to support you? If you can, tell them first. That way they will be able to help you deal with other people's possibly less positive reactions. If you don't feel that anyone you know will be sympathetic, consider contacting a counselling centre or a telephone helpline. It is not easy to go it alone – you may find just being able to talk about your situation openly and in confidence will lessen your feelings of isolation and panic.

PARTNERS

Unplanned pregnancy can put a searchlight on your relationship – spotlighting how well the relationship is going, how you communicate, and how you both deal with a crisis. If the relationship is strong, then the experience may bring you even closer; alternatively, you could realize you don't know this person as well as you thought and be very disturbed by their reaction.

How you and your partner cope will depend on the history, length and nature of your relationship. You may feel your partner is central in making the decision or you may want to make up your own mind. You are likely to feel a lot less pressured if the decision is a joint one, with the proviso that he will support you whatever choice you make. Even if you choose abortion, it can be very reassuring to know your partner would have stood by you had you continued the pregnancy. You will then be able to see your decision as a real choice rather than something you were pushed into.

It is very difficult, especially in an established relationship, when your partner's wishes are directly opposed to yours. (We will explore some of the issues around conflict with partners in Chapter Three, 'Conflict with Yourself and with Others'.) However, even if you are not in total opposition, there can still be problems. You may expect your partner to share your feelings and feel very angry if he doesn't. If he is unemotional and detached and can't understand why abortion isn't an easy choice, this may be very upsetting for you. You may feel that he is self-centred, unable to give you the support you need and is shirking his responsibility. You might be frustrated because he is unable to talk about his emotions or is taking out his fears about commitment and fatherhood on you. You could end up fighting instead of talking or feel there is an unbridgeable gulf between you.

During this time you could both also be considering some big questions about the relationship. Do you have a future together? Do you have the same priorities? Do you want to be parents and, if so, when? How will having a child affect the relationship? How will you feel about him if you have an abortion?

We live in a society in which men are brought up to go for what they want and put their own needs first. Men are not encouraged to show their vulnerabilities and not usually taught how to look after other people's emotional needs. Your pregnancy will present a big challenge to your partner. He may meet the challenge very well or he may flounder under the impact. Some men are quite terrified of pregnancy and its emotional complications. It is something which is outside their experience and, therefore, seems outside their control. He may be angry because he knows, in the end, it is your decision but it's one which will also affect his life. He may be very distressed about the pregnancy but not know how to express it, or feel he doesn't have the right to. He may feel very rejected by you not wanting to have his child. If your partner is in a panic, it is unlikely he will be able to give any valuable support until he has addressed his own fears.

It may help to understand your partner's feelings but this doesn't mean you should be the one looking after them or that you should accept unreasonable behaviour. It may be useful for him to get support from other people - as long as you feel it's all right for him to tell them about your pregnancy and they will keep it confidential. Some women have felt angry with a partner who has rushed off to tell his friends or family without their permission.

Some couples decide that an unplanned pregnancy is something they want to keep between themselves – especially if they are considering termination. If you do decide not to tell anyone but your partner then it will be important that he can give you the support you need, which will mean listening to and respecting your feelings even if they are different from his own.

You also both need to be clear about who is taking responsibility for the decision. Is the decision open to negotiation or have you already decided what you want to do? If you do want to fully involve your partner in the decision you also need to decide what you're going to do if you disagree (see Chapter Three, 'Conflict with Yourself and with Others'). If you want to continue the pregnancy you should establish whether this is dependent on his agreement and support or whether you're prepared to carry on alone. You may hope he will come round eventually – and he might, but don't bank on it.

If you have an abortion you could both be anxious about how this may affect your relationship. The more you are able to talk without blaming each other or feeling threatened, the more likely it is your relationship will survive.

If he leaves it up to you to decide, make sure you are not in a position where you're trying to guess what his feelings are and what he wants. You need to know where you stand and whether your expectations are realistic. Respecting your wishes is very different from opting out altogether.

Being honest with each other may not be easy but in the long run it could save you a lot of pain. It could also involve you facing up to the limitations of your relationship and may even end with you splitting up . If you are facing a termination and the end of a relationship, this double loss could be particularly painful – but you could take comfort in the thought that someone who can't support you through this is unlikely to be able to offer much as a lifetime companion.

It is unlikely that your partner can be totally objective in this situation. If he supports your decision to continue the pregnancy, he will have to deal with the emotional and financial pressures of being a father. If you decide to have an abortion, you may be hurt by his obvious relief or you may feel you have to justify to him why you don't want his child. All this need not damage your relationship – if you have a strong commitment to making it work, you will be able to find constructive ways of supporting each other.

If you have decided to have an abortion and are worried that your partner may pressurize you into keeping the baby, you may decide not to tell him. You may also choose not to tell him because it's not his child or because you want to protect him or because you feel he will be unable to support you. Usually, women who keep the pregnancy a secret have very valid reasons for doing so. If you are in a violent relationship you may be very frightened of your partner's reaction. Whatever the reason, you will have to make sure that your partner doesn't find out by confiding only in people you trust and by checking out the confidentiality of your GP or anyone else you go to for help. You may also need to weigh up your reasons against the strain of keeping the whole thing a secret.

PARENTS

How big a role your parents or family play in this decision will depend on your age and your degree of financial and emotional dependence on them. If you are young and still living at home, then your parents' attitude could be very important. We will look at specific issues for young women in Chapter Three, 'Conflict with Yourself and with Others'.

It is possible to have high expectations that your family will be there for you in times of trouble. This can be true – some women find their mothers and sisters (and occasionally fathers and brothers) are very understanding, especially if you are facing the pregnancy without a partner. However, your family may have equally high expectations of you. An unplanned pregnancy can make your parents feel as though they have failed. They may also be part of a generation which never talked about sex, where unmarried mothers were a scandal, and abortion totally taboo. It may take them a while to realize that things have changed. They may be frightened for you and assume you will have an awful time, whatever you do, or they may be angry with you for letting them down.

If you have decided to have a termination and you know your parents disapprove strongly of abortion, or don't know about your sex life, then you may choose not to tell them – if you can avoid it. In fact, your parents' disapproval and your culture's or community's attitude to single parents can sometimes be a major factor in your choice to have a termination.

It can be painful to withhold this information from your family. You may also torment yourself by imagining their disapproval if they found out the truth. However, it is also important to accept that you have a right to your own life – and this includes a right to privacy and to make different choices from your parents.

If you want to continue the pregnancy you may need to ask your parents for financial or practical support – and if you are reliant on or are still living with them, it can put you in a tricky position if they refuse. However, not many parents would wish to be permanently estranged from their daughter and grandchild and you may find that initially hostile reactions will soften considerably over time.

You may also want your parents' support if you have an abortion – and you could need their financial help if you want to go privately. You may find that their wish to help and protect you outweighs any negative feelings they may have about the pregnancy – or they could give you a very hard time. Even the most tolerant parents can find it hard to accept their daughter as a sexual being. This is especially true if you have no history of discussing your private life with them.

Your parents may believe that they know better than you what you should do. They may have invested a lot of their hopes and dreams in you and find it difficult to accept that they cannot influence your life. If your parents have high expectations of you, they could be horrified at your choice to be a single mother and feel that you are throwing your life away. If your own mother has spent her life bringing up children, she may feel resentful of or threatened by your decision to have an abortion. Your parents may feel you are depriving them of grandchildren.

If you are unsure how your parents will react it is a good idea to find an ally in the family. This could be a brother or sister you are close to, an aunt, grandmother or close family friend. Your ally can help you stand up for what you want and challenge your parents if they are being unreasonable. It may also be easier for them, rather than for you, to listen to how your parents are feeling.

Your parents are more likely to be helpful if they see you as an adult who has the right to make her own decisions. If this is the case, they will be less tempted to swamp you with advice or see the pregnancy as their problem rather than yours.

FRIENDS

Friends tend to be less emotionally involved in your decision than your partner or family and may be able to offer you more objective support. Your close friends may be the ones who you can talk to most rationally about your decision. They can hold your hand while you're waiting for your pregnancy test result, and provide moral support at the clinic or hospital. Your friends may have been through the same situation themselves or at least have a good idea of how you may be feeling.

Friends, like your family and partner, will also have their own opinions and advice – but a good friend will listen to what you want rather than impose their own ideas. Be wary of anyone (whether it's friends or family) who comes out with anything similar to the following comments:

Mary had an abortion and felt suicidal for about a year.

You wouldn't want to deprive me of being an uncle/grandmother/ godmother, would you?

You can't look after yourself. What makes you think you could look after a child?

You'll never find a man if you have a baby on your own.

I don't know how you can be so calm. If I was you I'd want to jump under a bus.

Believe me, I know you better than you know yourself and I know exactly how you will feel.

All these comments may be very well-meaning, but they say more about the other person's fears and fixed ideas than they say about you. Try not to be undermined by heavy-handed advice. If you can, ask clearly for what you want. This may be help in reaching a decision or just added reassurance that you're doing the right thing. It would also be helpful if the people around you didn't assume that they know what you'll be feeling: and don't expect everyone to be immediately sympathetic – it may take them a while to come to terms with their own feelings about your pregnancy.

YOUR GP

If you have a good relationship with your GP, then you might want his/her help in making your decision. Your GP may also have good information about the different options available to you and could even help you talk with your partner or family.

However, your GP may not have the skills to do this. Some GPs don't have the time or inclination to listen to their patients' problems. Your doctor may also have strong personal feelings or moral objections to abortion – s/he may not agree that you have the right to make your own decision and may disapprove or make assumptions about your lifestyle.

Some women have felt undermined by their GP's patronizing attitudes. We will look in more detail at being assertive with your GP and other professionals in the section, 'Negotiating the System', in Chapter Five, p. 84.

Remember, you don't need to inform your GP if you want a charity or private-sector termination. You may also be worried by confidentiality in your doctor's surgery, especially if you live in a small community or you are keeping the termination a secret from the people close to you. If you do inform your doctor, details of your pregnancy and termination will go on your medical files. If you are worried about who has access to your file and whether your GP will treat any information as strictly confidential, then check this out with them before you disclose anything personal.

COUNSELLORS

If you have problems making your decision, feel very anxious about it or have little support from the people around you, then it can be very useful to talk over your situation with a counsellor.

All the abortion charities offer 'counselling only' appointments – this means you can arrange a termination at a later date but there will be no pressure for you to do this. They will be very concerned that the abortion is entirely your decision, and will also support your right to continue the pregnancy.

You may also be able to see a counsellor through your GP or Family Planning Clinic. If you are under twenty-six you can go to a Brook Advisory Centre; alternatively, the British Association of Counselling (BAC) or your local Citizens Advice Bureau (CAB) should be able to provide you with a list of free or low-cost counselling services in your area (*see* Help and Information, p. 174).

A counsellor is not there to make up your mind for you or to solve all your problems, but is trained to help you see your situation more objectively so that you can make the best decision. S/he can help you explore difficult issues and encourage you to express your feelings to the extent that it feels safe for you to do so.

Good counsellors should not make you feel judged or impose their own codes of morals or beliefs on you. In order for you to benefit from counselling, you will need to know that the session is confidential and that this person has no vested interest in your continuing the pregnancy or having an abortion.

The counsellor should also be able to support and affirm the decision you make as well as helping you reach it. Counselling is not helpful if you feel the person is going to undermine your decision or if you believe they have the power to withhold the termination if you act in the wrong way. You should not feel worried about having to make the right impression.

Many women have had very positive experiences of counselling at the charity pregnancy advisory services. The counsellors there are familiar with the issues surrounding unplanned pregnancy; it can be very reassuring to have your feelings met with respect and understanding and to be told you're not mad or stupid or unnatural. Counsellors will also see you with your partner or a member of your family if this is useful and will usually see partners on their own if that is what you want.

Of course, counsellors are human beings, not saints, and you may find that a particular counsellor is unhelpful. It could be a personality clash or that their way of working isn't useful to you.

You may also feel that the counsellor has little or no understanding of your racial or religious background or culture.

If you are black or Asian you may feel that a white counsellor cannot understand your experience or you might be concerned that they will make racist assumptions about you. These are valid concerns – and as most services will be white-dominated it may not be possible to see a counsellor from your own culture. You could choose to get support from a community organization or a culturally based counselling service (*see* Help and Information, p. 174).

However, it is also part of any counsellor's job to be aware of the needs of women from different cultural, ethnic and religious backgrounds and you have the right to expect a good service from anyone you see. So, if you are not happy with the counsellor, ask to see someone else. It may be daunting to criticize them, but if the agency is committed to helping all women they should respect your wishes.

OTHER PEOPLE'S ATTITUDES TO YOUR PREGNANCY

We can all be affected by the way society views women, motherhood and abortion and this is a time when you may be particularly vulnerable to other people's views or assumptions about you. We still don't have the right in law to freely choose to have an abortion; many people still do not regard it as a valid choice. While motherhood is seen as something the majority of women want, we also get strong messages of what we should be like in order to be good mothers.

The media image of the perfect mother is white, middle-class, married, not too young or too old and preferably well-off and angelic. Most of us don't live in a Fairy Liquid commercial, and not everyone will have the same equality of choice in making a decision about their pregnancy.

Some women still have to struggle to prove their right to be mothers at all. If you are disabled, HIV positive, lesbian or single, then being a parent can also involve a long fight against prejudice and bigotry. The joys of motherhood can also be severely undermined by inadequate housing, low wages and meagre benefits, discrimination and lousy childcare facilities. For some women abortion will be a financial necessity.

If you are a black woman, you may be suspicious of the white medical establishment's motives in offering you a termination. It is certainly true that some black and working-class women have been pressurized by doctors into accepting sterilization or injectable contraceptives after the abortion. If you are made to feel as though you would be an unfit mother, that you have too many children, or that you wouldn't have a lot to give up if you had the baby, then it will be difficult for you to see abortion as something you can choose on your own terms.

Recognizing and understanding the possible pressures and discrimination you may be facing from the outside world can also help you take control of your decision. If you make a choice based on what you want, rather than what is expected of you, then it is likely that it will be the right one.

CHAPTER THREE

CONFLICT WITH YOURSELF AND WITH OTHERS

———

In this chapter we will be considering some specific situations, or ways you might be feeling, which may make the decision about your pregnancy a particularly difficult or complex one.

DEALING WITH AMBIVALENCE

It is common to feel confused or unsure at some point in your decision-making process. Even if you're fairly clear what you want to do, there may be days when you have doubts or think about the possibilities of choosing a different option. But some women get completely trapped by their inability to make a decision. Does this sound familiar? You wake up in the morning and you know you want an abortion; by that evening you're convinced you can't go through with it and you'll keep the baby – you lie awake all night worrying about finances, family and support. You then consider adoption, reject the idea and by the next morning you're back where you started. Only you know that's not the answer, so you end up feeling like a mouse on a wheel, going over the same information without being able to come to a decision and stick to it. A few days of this are enough to drive you up the wall with frustration, never mind the lack of sleep and the general level of anxiety.

It could be that all the options seem equally depressing. You may know instinctively you don't want an abortion but equally be lost as to how you're going to cope as a parent at this time in your life. If you do feel this, then you are in a no-win situation. It makes sense that if all the options appear equally dire then you will be reluctant to make a decision at all. What are the positive aspects of each choice? They may not be easy to find but it is important to consider them. If you convince yourself that you will lose out whatever you do, then this can become a self-fulfilling prophecy.

There can be many reasons why it is hard to decide. One might be that it's bringing up painful feelings for you. It could be that you've always associated having an abortion with a sense of failure or that you are uneasy about the future of your relationship. It may be that there are advantages in either decision which make it equally difficult for you to make a choice. Perhaps you've wanted a child for some time but have just started a new and demanding job; you've begun a course you've wanted to do for ages; or you are in the first months of a new relationship.

Give yourself a realistic deadline for making up your mind. Rather than seeing the days and weeks stretching ahead into a panicky blur, sit down and work out how much time you need: a few days – a week – possibly a couple of weeks if the pregnancy is early?

Now you have set your time limit, allow yourself a day or two to just express your feelings – whatever they are. It may help to break the wheel of indecision if you can stop pushing yourself into making the right choice. Spend some time just resting, or having a good cry, or doing something you enjoy – whatever feels right.

Once you have confronted the most painful part of the decision, you may find things become clearer. You might also realize that you have a history of finding it hard to make decisions, or a conviction that whatever you decide will be wrong. Are there other times in the past when you couldn't make up your mind? Look back and work out what helped. Was it useful to talk to other people, or do they just cloud the issue? Why do you doubt your ability to make the right decisions for yourself? What are you most frightened of? Are your fears realistic?

Try not to see yourself as a ditherer but as someone who puts a lot of thought into things. What we said about trusting yourself in Chapter Two, 'Making Your Decision', is very important here. For some women, deciding about a pregnancy is the first or most difficult major choice in their adult lives.

Many more women feel that they have made the right choices about their pregnancy than believe they have made a mistake. Even women who have found abortion a painful decision usually say they would do the same if they could turn the clock back; this also applies to women who have chosen to go ahead with the pregnancy. Allow yourself to have some regrets. Even though it's important to look at the positive, it's just as important not to try to make the perfect choice. It probably doesn't exist.

If you talk through and explore these issues, eventually the way forward will be clearer. If you feel very stuck or find it daunting to explore your feelings on your own, then it could help to spend time with a trusted friend, or with a sympathetic counsellor who may be able to help you clarify what seems to be a jumble of contradictions. Pregnancy counsellors will be experienced in dealing with the fact that time is short and something has to be resolved one way or the other. They have talked to many women facing a similar dilemma.

You can see a counsellor, whether you decide on an NHS or private termination, are considering adoption or keeping the baby (*see* Help and Information, p. 174). If you need more than one session this should be available, too. Putting all this work into sorting out what you want is never wasted – it should help you to feel more confident about your choice and your ability to cope with the future.

CONFLICT WITH PARTNERS

Facing unplanned pregnancy on your own may be very lonely and frightening, but being part of a couple can bring its own problems. In Chapter Two, 'Making Your Decision', we looked at your partner's role in your decision and some of the issues and problems that might arise. But what happens when your wishes are diametrically opposed to your partner's? It may be that you want to continue the pregnancy but your partner doesn't, or that you want an abortion and he is very against the idea.

This is particularly difficult if you are in a committed relationship or married, because your partner will be an important part of your life and therefore losing the relationship won't be something you will contemplate lightly. In a way, it is a 'no-compromise' situation – you either have the baby or have an abortion. You may both feel trapped in the situation, furious with the other person and amazed that they see the future so differently from you.

In the end, of course, it should be your choice. Your partner may try to, but cannot ultimately pressurize you into having a baby or an abortion without your consent. However, if you risk losing the relationship or you cannot manage without your partner's support, this may not feel like a real choice.

Where the man is the sole earner, this can lead to his feeling he has the right to make decisions for the whole family. It can be hard sometimes to challenge the person who pays all the bills. If you are home looking after two children and get pregnant again, you may very much want another child but feel unable to continue without your husband's support. You could be furious that your partner is bullying you into having a termination but equally reluctant to take the risk of bringing up three children alone – or with a resentful father.

There can be many reasons why your partner would prefer you to have an abortion rather than continue with the pregnancy. He could feel that the time isn't right and it's important to wait till you're more financially secure. He may think that you previously had a 'bargain' – that you both didn't want children – and can't understand why you are feeling different now you are actually pregnant. You may discover he's not as committed to you as you thought, or he's just plain terrified of being a father.

The way in which you begin to negotiate the situation will, of course, depend on the sort of relationship you have. If the relationship is a good one, if you respect each other's feelings and are able to communicate quite easily, then you have a solid basis to work from. If things are going wrong between you, then an unplanned pregnancy will dramatically highlight these problems. What can be frightening in this situation is if you believe that, if you have the abortion he wants, you will be so resentful that it will destroy the relationship anyway and that, if you have the child he doesn't want, the same thing will happen.

Perhaps the first thing to establish is whether there is room for negotiation. If it is impossible to talk constructively, if your partner continues to be abusive or persistently disregards your feelings, you may have to take a long, hard look at whether you want to live with this person. If you do, you might need to accept that your reasons for staying in the relationship outweigh your wish to make your own choices. It may also be the case that your partner is not simply being an inconsiderate bully and does care about your feelings, but simply refuses to contemplate the idea of having a child at this time.

Sometimes, it is difficult but necessary to separate your feelings about the pregnancy from your feelings about the relationship. To do this, it is useful to talk to someone outside – a close friend or a counsellor – to really establish what you want. It might also be useful to ask yourself the following questions:

- Am I prepared to continue the pregnancy alone?
- If I do continue, how likely is it he will stick by me?
- If we stay together, what sort of expectations do I have? Will he make a good father?
- If we split up what sort of relationship do I want him to have with the child? Can I expect any financial or emotional support?
- How will I feel about him if I have the abortion? Will we need joint counselling? Will we split up anyway? Is this relationship really important to me?
- What do I feel about his reasons for wanting me to have an abortion? Are they valid? Can we talk them through together?

Once you have answered these questions for yourself – and discussed some of them with your partner – you should have a clearer idea about what your expectations are, and how likely they are to be fulfilled.

You need to be clear about the circumstances in which you're prepared to have a baby. If the pregnancy is very important, you may decide to go ahead with or without his support. If you decide this, then you have made it clear that you are not open to having an abortion. Your partner may well be angry at this, but you are not trapping him by your decision – he can choose how much, if at all, he wants to be involved.

It might be unacceptable to you to be a single parent or just impossible on a practical and financial level. In this situation, it could help to see that an abortion is still your choice, but a choice based on the fact that your partner can't give you what you want. Some women in this situation have a termination but finish the relationship as well.

The pressure and responsibility involved in resolving an unplanned pregnancy may cast harsh new light on a relationship: you may feel disenchanted and let down by his behaviour, or you may start thinking about what you want from the future and realize that he will not be part of it. It is difficult to resuscitate a relationship where there has been a total breakdown of trust and understanding. You may resent him for getting you 'into trouble', and because it is you – not him – who is paying the price, he may feel blamed and excluded. Or he may abandon you. Or he may suspect you of deliberately getting pregnant in order to 'trap' him. A previously satisfactory relationship could suddenly explode with bitter mutual recriminations.

If you do want to keep the relationship, but both want different things, then it's going to be hard work. It might not be easy to be honest with each other. You may feel apologetic because you had assumed you wouldn't want a child at this stage. He may feel guilty because he can't support you. But however painful, it is more constructive to face the reality now than trying to please the other person and making a decision you'll regret.

In any discussion between you there should be a balance

between being clear about what you want and also being prepared to listen to and to respect the other person's point of view. It might be useful to consider the following points when you are trying to discuss the pregnancy together:

- **How do you feel about each other right now?** Bear in mind that it will be very difficult to discuss the issue rationally if you're both furiously angry. If you keep having rows, then maybe you need a little time apart – or negotiate a truce.
- **Be prepared to listen**. Give each other some uninterrupted space to say what you each feel and why. Every time either of you want to jump in and say 'Yes, but...' bite your tongue. Make sure the time is equal.
- **Talk about your own feelings, not the other person's.** It's very tempting to tell your partner what a wonderful father he'd make and very irritating if he tells you you'll regret it if you have the baby now.
- **Be as honest as you dare.** Try not to fudge the issues in order to protect the other person's feelings. He's a grown-up – let him look after his own!
- **Really let each other talk about what your fears are**. If he is anxious about settling down or being a father, let him express this. If you feel you will resent him bitterly if you have an abortion, try to be clear about this.

Not everyone finds it easy to talk clearly and assertively about their emotions. As women we are often taught to be accommodating and not to stick up for what we want. Men, on the other hand, are often taught not to express their emotions at all and may have great difficulty talking honestly about how they feel.

This isn't to say that everyone falls neatly into those patterns; challenging and honest discussion may already be part of your relationship. If it isn't, then don't have unrealistic expectations of each other – it may be helpful to see a counsellor together who will help facilitate a more constructive exploration of your situation.

Whatever you decide to do, it could be painful to let go of your dream of shared happiness. You may desperately wish that your partner is as excited about having a child as you are and feel cheated when all he can do is panic and worry about himself.

It is justifiable to be angry with a partner who is selfish, immature or unable to accept a different lifestyle. It is tempting to spend a lot of emotional energy trying to force someone to change or punishing them for not being the person you want them to be. You need to be realistic about what your partner can give to you. This does not mean you should be an emotional doormat. In fact, the more you quash your anger and ignore what you want, the more likely you are to spend years feeling resentful or to turn the anger in on yourself. If you are honest about your individual fears and concerns, then it could be easier to negotiate a decision which doesn't leave one of you feeling resentful and abused.

Perhaps your partner's main fear is that he will not be able to cope financially if you have a child and give up work. A compromise may be that you work part-time or continue to work with the help of a childminder. You might also need to look at your future plans and decide whether these are individual or shared ones. What is your partner frightened of giving up, if he becomes a father? Are his fears justified? If he believes you are taking his feelings and doubts seriously, then it may be easier for him to support you in continuing the pregnancy.

If, on the other hand, you accept his argument that it is too difficult to have a child now, where does that leave your future together? If this is the wrong time to have a baby, when will be the right time? If having a child is important to you, you will need to believe in his commitment to creating the right circumstances. It may not be enough to be fobbed off with vague promises – you might want to spend time working out a realistic agenda, and need to be clear with each other how important having children is in your list of priorities.

It will be extremely important for your partner to acknowledge and support your feelings if you decide to terminate your pregnancy. You could need reassurance that it is not something that will be dismissed once you've had the operation. If the decision is painful, then it will continue to affect your relationship – you will probably need to keep talking about it and possibly make a commitment to joint counselling if your feelings remain unresolved.

The opposite scenario, where your partner wants you to have the baby and you want an abortion, has different implications. If you continue the pregnancy, you can choose to do so with or without your partner's support; he cannot, however, have a child on your behalf. It is a very disturbing implication for yourself and the child if your only reason for having a baby is because of pressure from your partner.

It may be that your reasons for not wanting the baby are to do mainly with your career or lifestyle; it might be possible in these circumstances to agree that your partner is responsible for most of the childcare. Society has been quite slow in accepting that men can bring up their children, but it is much more sensible to work out an arrangement which suits you both rather than sticking to a rigid tradition. However, you will both need to be clear that this is a workable solution and that your partner is committed to being the primary parent. You will also need to decide what your role will be in the child's life and what positive things you will gain by going ahead with the pregnancy. It is unlikely that you will want to go through nine months of carrying a child and a lifetime of being a mother without being sure that you are doing this for yourself and not because someone else wants you to.

It is important to be clear about what you expect from each other and what is on offer. We are bombarded with so many romantic myths about relationships that sometimes it is very hard to be realistic about your own. How do you both see yourselves as parents? Is the childcare going to be shared or is one of you going to take most of the responsibility? How emotionally involved do you want your partner to be?

When we stop wanting the same things a relationship can become a battleground or a desert of non-communication. None of the options open to you may seem particularly easy, especially if it ends up being a choice between your pregnancy and your relationship. Even if you persuade your partner to support you in having the baby, you may still have doubts that his support and the relationship will last.

You should not feel guilty for sticking up for what you want – neither should you blame yourself if you choose to go with what your partner wants nor if the relationship ends. Making the right choice will involve accepting that the circumstances are not ideal, and you may need to mourn the loss of what might have been.

CONFLICT WITH PARENTS

If you are a teenager still living at home, you may be feeling particularly frightened and alone. Telling your family that you are pregnant can be very difficult when you are still dependent on them and living under their control. Maybe this is the first time they have had to face up to your adult sexuality – perhaps they didn't even know that you were not still a virgin. They may see this 'proof' of your sexual activity as wilful misbehaviour or as a sign that they have failed as parents in letting you go 'off the rails'. Teenage sex is often very frightening to parents: after all, to them you are still a little girl, yet here you are showing that you have furiously active hormones, vivid curiosity, and desire for close physical intimacy and for love – just like them.

As if this were not hard enough, parents always want to know why you have got pregnant; this is a difficult question to answer. The younger you are, the smaller the chance that you were using birth control at the time of conception. We all take risks, adults as well as teenagers, but again there may have been particular problems which stopped you using contraception. Maybe the prospect of pregnancy seemed so unreal that you couldn't believe it would happen to you; maybe you didn't know where to go or who to ask for help; maybe you weren't expecting to have sex. Most girls are raised with the idea that they should make other people happy, even at their own expense; maybe you didn't want to inconvenience your boyfriend, or you didn't want to appear unromantic or calculating, or he refused to wear a condom. Maybe you were scared your family or friends would find the pills or diaphragm, and it was important to you to keep your sex life secret. Maybe you do have a method of contraception, but you don't like it and so have been using it haphazardly. Maybe part of you is tempted to get pregnant to prove your fertility, or to stop your boyfriend from leaving you, or to have someone truly your own to care for.

Whatever the circumstances of your pregnancy, it can send some very powerful messages to your family and friends. Pregnancy may seem a way out of the family home, or it could be a way of punishing those around you, or asserting your independence and maturity. Your parents will be having difficulties adjusting to your adult sexuality: they may blame you, themselves or each other, and this anger can disrupt the whole family, making you feel worse than ever.

There are various reasons why you have to involve your parents in plans for your pregnancy. If you are thinking of continuing the pregnancy, you will need to know how much support they will give you and whether you can carry on living at home. If you want an abortion, you may need their consent (if you are under 16) and possibly their financial support. Even if you'd prefer not to tell them, it might be too difficult to find a convincing alibi for weight gain, morning sickness, or time spent at the hospital.

Most parents, however shocked or upset, do rally round to support their daughters through unplanned pregnancy. But what happens when you tell your parents and they are angry instead of supportive? What happens if you want the baby and they are insistent that you should have an abortion – or they don't approve of abortion and put pressure on you to continue the pregnancy? It can be very frightening if your parents oppose or don't approve of your decision and it can highlight all sorts of other problems in the family. If you are young and dependent upon them, your parents may feel they know what is best for you and could try hard to influence your choice if it is different from what they want.

You might feel that your parents have the power to force you to have an abortion or to continue the pregnancy against your will. This may not be true, but your parents can make things difficult for you by withholding financial support or by bullying you into accepting what they want. If you and your parents reach total stalemate, if they refuse to listen to what you want or are violent or abusive, then it will be important for you to seek help either within or outside the family.

Try to find another adult who will be on your side. This could be a sympathetic teacher, family friend, social worker or an advice worker at a youth-counselling centre. Think about who will be your ally within the family as well – it might be a good idea to talk to an elder brother or sister, aunt or grandparent – and ask them to help you negotiate with your parents.

This is not to imply that most parents are monsters who have no regard for their children's wishes. Your parents will be having a difficult time, too, and will probably be struggling to do what they believe is right for you. Your pregnancy will be a big challenge for them. They may still see you as a little girl and here you are, confronting them with the fact that you are a young adult with a sex life. If you want to have a baby then they may be in for an even bigger shock – trying to imagine someone they still see as their child as a mother in her own right.

Becoming an adult is also not something that happens overnight. Adolescence can be a confusing time because you will be testing your independence and starting to build your own life, but you may still be very emotionally dependent on your parents, and want to be approved of and protected by them. You may also be furiously angry with them if they continue to treat you like a child or resentful if they don't respect you or seem to ignore what you want.

If you want to go ahead with the pregnancy, you should think carefully about your reasons. You may be very angry that your parents want you to have an abortion; keeping the baby can be a way of standing up to them and stating you are a separate person and that they cannot make choices for you. You may also see an abortion quite differently from your parents. If you are young, with little experience of life, it is easier to have a very idealistic view of the world. This view could include very romantic ideas about having children; abortion could seem to be a very cruel choice – or one where you are shirking your responsibility. Your friends may also have very strong opinions on the subject and you might worry they will disapprove of you if you don't have the baby. It is very natural to feel this, but you should also take into account that having a child is a huge responsibility and could change your life quite drastically.

It is important to take back the decision for yourself. You are a young adult and you have rights and feelings of your own. Being angry about being pushed about by your parents is not in itself a good enough reason to have a child. What are your other reasons? You may feel that this baby belongs to you and you want very much to be a mother. You will need to weigh this up against other important things in your life like your job, or your education, or simply the freedom to have a good time with your friends. Having a child can be very rewarding, but if you are very young it is also likely to be a struggle. You need to be clear about what support is available and how you will cope on a practical level.

Sometimes parents (especially mothers) will want you to have an abortion because they simply don't feel you are grown up enough to look after a child and that they will end up doing all the work. This is a valid point; if you are determined to go ahead, you will need to be confident that you will be able to cope. How do you prove you are mature enough to be a mother? One way is to show your parents you have really thought about your decision. You should try and come up with responsible answers to their questions, rather than feeling resentful that they are asking them. They are less likely to oppose you if you convince them you've taken their fears into account. Have you thought about where you will live and what you will live on? Have you considered the problems of living at home with the baby? Have you a clear idea what's involved in being a parent? If you have, then you will have an easier job reassuring them that they won't be bringing up your baby for you.

It may be that your parents are still very protective of you. They want the best for you. They worry that if you have a child now you will lose out on job opportunities or all the freedoms associated with being young. Sometimes parents are very unsubtle in telling us that they know what is best for us. It doesn't always mean they are wrong. Your parents have first-hand experience of what it's like to have children. You may feel that they are just trying to put you off by saying you won't be a good mother, but it is important to also consider seriously what you might be giving up.

There needs to be a willingness on both sides to listen and to respect the other person's feelings. Dismissing their arguments out of hand will only wind them up. Let them see that you've thought about the future, too. Try to see what the world and your pregnancy looks like from their position. That doesn't mean you're more likely to do what they want, but it should give you a better understanding of what their anxieties are and what you can realistically expect from them. Just as your parents cannot legally force you to have an abortion, you cannot force them to be supportive. It could seem as though you don't have a real choice if they refuse to let you live at home or won't help you financially.

If you are determined to continue the pregnancy and you have a basically good relationship with your parents, then it is likely that they will come round to supporting you – even if their initial reaction is one of shock and anger. **But it is important to weigh up what is on offer when you make your decision, and work out whether it is possible to be independent from them.** Is it feasible for you to leave home? Can you live with another member of your family? Can you afford to live on your own or with your partner? When you are young you are less likely to have a lot of money. If you decide that you can't cope without their support, then you may choose to have a termination. This could be a painful decision, but you should not feel it is your fault. In fact, it's very brave to be realistic about your circumstances rather than closing your eyes and hoping for the best.

Remember, you won't always be dependent on somebody else. You have your whole future to look forward to; in a few years you will be free to make your own decisions about your relationships and having children. You might, however, continue to feel very angry with your parents and sad about the abortion. If you do, make sure you have access to people outside the home who are sympathetic; close friends may be able to give you support, or you could think about talking to a counsellor at a youth advisory service.

If, on the other hand, you want an abortion and your parents disapprove, you will also need support. It is possible that your parents will put pressure on you to have the child, but it is harder to demand someone has a baby if they obviously do not want one. They may not actually forbid you to have the termination, but express their disapproval by punishing you for getting pregnant.

Some parents still believe that an unplanned pregnancy outside marriage is a disgrace. They will remember, and may still be living by, their own parents' beliefs and attitudes. Sex is usually a taboo subject in the family, and there can be more pressure on daughters than sons not to flout convention. How you deal with your parents' disapproval will depend on your relationship with them. Sometimes the anger and disapproval will be shortlived, but if it does continue you need to be able to protect yourself from it.

Remember, by lashing out at you they are expressing their own fears but you don't have to believe everything they say about you. Talk to your friends or to a sympathetic teacher or someone else who can see things from where you are standing. If things get very bad then you could see a counsellor with your parents. Their anger and disapproval could also be about wider issues, not just the pregnancy: fear of you growing up; fear of losing you and the control over your life; anxiety that they will be to blame if you make a mess of your life; feeling very threatened if you make different choices from the ones they made.

Generally, if you are in conflict with someone else it is

impossible to negotiate when anger and hurt are in the air. If your parents are intent on punishing you – or you, them – it is unlikely you will be able to have very constructive discussions about your future. **If you make it clear that you can understand their position, it may be easier for them to try and understand yours.** They need to fully realize that your decision is not made as a punishment or an aggressive act towards them, but something you want for yourself.

FERTILITY CRISES

Making a decision about an unplanned pregnancy can have particular significance if you see it as your last chance to have a child. In this situation you're not just making a decision whether to have this child but whether you are going to be a mother at all.

One of the advantages of being older is that we tend to gain confidence about making decisions without feeling bad about society's pressure or approval. However, you could feel that there is more – not less – pressure on you to 'settle down' and have a child. Your pregnancy may also bring up quite intense and sometimes contradictory feelings about yourself as a woman and what place – if any – children have in your life.

First, let's look at what we mean by 'last chance'. It is true that your fertility will start to decline as you get older. If a fertile couple are having sex at the right time of the month for a year then it has been estimated that 80–90 per cent of women under the age of thirty will get pregnant. From thirty-five onwards 75 per cent will still be successful, but after forty many women's fertility will decline quite quickly, so that by forty-five only about 10–20 per cent of women will be able to conceive and carry a child. Of course, statistics can't tell you much about your own fertility. Many women do have children in their early forties so, if you do have a termination in your late thirties, it doesn't automatically mean you will never be a mother. But it may be important to acknowledge that you cannot rely on your fertility as you get older.

However, fertility may not be the only issue. If you have a termination now, are your circumstances likely to change much over the next few years? If you are single or not in a committed relationship, is it likely you will find a partner who wants to have children? You may be quite happy about being single, but do you want to bring up a child on your own? Of course, having a relationship and a child do not need to go hand in hand. Nowadays more single women, both lesbian and heterosexual, are choosing to have children without a male partner. However, as this pregnancy is unplanned, circumstances could make it difficult for you to continue. You could also be in a stable relationship where you are both unsure about whether you want to be parents.

Some women talk about being 'set in their ways' when they get older. You may have an established and enjoyable lifestyle and career and find the idea of a child very disruptive. You may have doubts about being an older parent and wonder whether you can cope with the demands of a baby, let alone a teenager! If you do have a good job and supportive friends, then continuing the pregnancy could seem a viable option. You would have to consider what you would lose in terms of freedom against what you would gain by being a mother.

You could be feeling apologetic about being pregnant if you are in your early forties. You might think you have less to offer than a younger woman. There is no reason why older women should not make good parents and lots of reasons why they do. Being mature and having done a lot in your life is valuable and can outweigh the energy of youth.

You may also be more anxious about the outcome of the pregnancy when you are older as the chance of miscarriage and of having a Down's Syndrome child does increase with age. The chance of having a child with Down's Syndrome is less than 1 in 1,000 from the ages of twenty to twenty-nine. This rises to 1 in 380 for a woman of thirty-five. By forty the chance is 1 in 100; by forty-three, 1 in 50. Again, statistics can't tell you the outcome of your pregnancy and if you are worried about Down's Syndrome, you can have an amniocentesis test (see section on Foetal Abnormality, p. 69).

There may also be a slightly increased risk of other complications during the pregnancy and birth as you get older but, if you are in good health and receive good medical care, the risks will remain relatively low. If your health and anxiety about the outcome of the pregnancy is a big factor in your decision, talk this over with a sympathetic doctor or other health professional.

Whatever choice you make, you may gain and lose something. Talk to many mothers and they will mourn the loss of time for themselves, the loss of their independence, not being able to lie-in in the morning, not being able to take an unexpected holiday or to learn a new skill. All these things are much harder to get when you are responsible for a child. However, if you have made a decision not to have children, you could feel sad about that, too. You may worry that you are missing out on one of life's major experiences or panic about being alone when you are older. If you want a child very much, then to decide it's not practically possible could be extremely painful.

Many people still believe that having a partner and a child is the only way to true happiness. If we look at the reality of women's lives behind the myth, we can see this patently isn't true. Although being a mother may be immensely satisfying, so too are friends, career, creativity, and the freedom to be only responsible for yourself.

If you do go ahead with a termination, allow yourself time to come to terms with the decision and the implications for you. They won't necessarily be negative – choosing not to have children may make you appreciate what's good and important about your lifestyle. If the decision is painful, then perhaps you could make a commitment to go for counselling afterwards in order to look at some of the wider issues and to help you to come to terms with the sense of loss.

If you already have children, you could also find it difficult to choose a termination which acknowledges your childbearing years are over. Some women feel very clear when their family is complete but others may be torn between practical considerations and a yearning to be pregnant again, especially if their children are growing up. You may have found that looking after your children when they were babies was the most rewarding part of being a mother; the sadness of terminating the pregnancy can get mixed up with the sadness of watching your children growing apart from you.

STRONG ANTI-ABORTION FEELINGS

You may be clear that abortion is not an option for you under any circumstances. This could be because of your personal philosophy, your religious beliefs, or your relationship with your culture or community. In this situation you will need to decide whether you can cope with keeping the baby or whether adoption is a viable alternative (see Chapter Seven, 'Choosing Motherhood' and Chapter Eight 'Adoption and Fostering').

However, it is not true that women who are anti-abortion never choose to have terminations – some of them do. Sometimes the devastating consequences of having a child can outweigh even the most profoundly held beliefs that abortion is wrong.

If you do hold strong anti-abortion views, and yet are considering termination, this puts you in a very difficult position. If you feel that what you are doing is morally wrong, how do you live with this? You may find that your views will change in the light of your pregnancy. Many people who are most vociferous about the evils of abortion have never had to deal with an unwanted pregnancy. You could be feeling guilty and surprised at yourself for seeing abortion as a way out of a terrible dilemma. It is more difficult to see a situation simply in abstract moral terms when it affects your life so profoundly.

On the other hand, a woman who chooses to continue the pregnancy because she really wants to have a child will have an easier time than someone who clearly does not want to be a mother but who cannot bring herself to have an abortion. If you feel desperately unhappy about being pregnant, how will this affect your relationship with the child? It will help if you are able to find some positive reasons for continuing the pregnancy. If you resent having the baby, then this is not going to make life easy for either of you. It is better to be honest with yourself now, rather than end up in a situation in which you feel trapped and helpless.

If you do decide to have a termination, it will be important for you to make peace with your conscience and your beliefs. Religions and cultures vary in their attitudes to abortion. Although most religions do not condone abortion, some religions accept that it is necessary under certain circumstances, and there are different views on the point at which the foetus becomes a separate life. However, everyone's relationship to their religion or culture is different. Within each religion, beliefs and levels of orthodoxy vary enormously and so will individual views about abortion. Even with a religion like Catholicism, which is strongly anti-abortion, there are some priests who are sympathetic to women who make this choice and who offer supportive counselling as well as granting absolution.

If you do belong to a church or religious community which disapproves of abortion, you could be feeling very lonely. You may not feel able to take the risk of telling anyone and you could be struggling to reach a decision on your own. You may need to examine your own beliefs in order to work out what is the most acceptable solution. If you do consider there is something sinful in abortion it could be useful to ask yourself the following questions:

- Is having an abortion wrong under any circumstances?
- Is terminating a foetus the same as killing a human being?
- At what point do you regard the foetus as a person?
- Is all life equally valuable including animal life, or is there an issue of quality?

The anti-abortion movement is notorious for using very emotive language and, if you share these beliefs, you may end up accusing yourself of 'murdering your baby' or 'killing your child'. Sometimes it is necessary to voice sentiments like this in order to register the pain involved in the abortion. However, continuing to see yourself as little short of a child murderer is immensely destructive. Whatever their beliefs, most people would see a difference between terminating a potential life and destroying an actual one.

Sin and retribution are part of most religious traditions, and if you do believe abortion is morally wrong it is possible you will feel the need to punish yourself. However, all religions also lay emphasis on compassion and forgiveness. Sometimes it is easier to be compassionate towards other people than towards yourself, but if *they* are deserving of your compassion, then so are *you*. Will you be able to forgive yourself? If you can't, what will you gain by a lifetime of self-punishment?

You may want the support of someone who shares your beliefs and, therefore, can fully understand the implications for you. This is a delicate situation because, if you talk to someone who is very disapproving of abortion, they could simply reinforce your negative feelings. However, it may be possible to find out through general discussion how sympathetic the person is likely to be. You could also find it useful to talk to a counsellor, who may not share your beliefs but will not be judgemental.

CHAPTER FOUR

DIFFICULT CIRCUMSTANCES

HARSH REALITY

In an ideal world, the only question you should have to ask yourself is 'Do I want this baby?' In the real world, you could feel as though you have no choice. You could feel it is impossible to continue the pregnancy because of health problems, financial difficulties or other pressures from family or community.

In this situation you can be made to feel guilty by the belief that, if you want the baby badly enough, you'll be able to cope somehow. This assumption is usually made by people who are not homeless, who have not tried to bring up a child in a bed and breakfast and who do not live on the poverty line. Women do have children in extraordinarily difficult circumstances, but it is important that you decide for yourself what is acceptable or unacceptable about your practical and financial situation.

For instance, you could have a live-in job you would lose, unsuitable accommodation, be recovering from an illness or already struggling with your mortgage. You may be part of a culture or a member of a religion which does not condone having children or sex outside marriage. You may be under a lot of pressure to keep the pregnancy a secret. In all these situations you will know very clearly what the practical reasons are for the termination. You may not have had to spend much time making a decision because the option of having a child is so difficult or down right impossible. It may seem that expressing your feelings about the termination is a luxury that you cannot afford.

Your main anxiety could be whether you will actually be able to get an abortion. If you cannot afford to go privately, you are dependent on the help of your GP and hospital consultants. This can be quite nerve-wracking, especially if you cannot make them understand how desperate your situation is, or if you feel that you will have to jump through hoops to show that you 'deserve' a termination (see section on 'Negotiating the System', p. 84). If you are having the abortion in secret, you could be lying awake at night trying to think up convincing alibis or praying that no one will find out.

Some women find that this sense of urgency gives them the strength to cope with the situation. If you feel you have no choice, then you are unlikely to have doubts that you are doing the right thing. However, once the operation is over, you could find that there is an emotional backlash. If you felt fairly powerless to begin with, how do you regain a sense of control? It will be important not to see the abortion as a personal failure. You may not have felt as though you had much control over your external circumstances but you do have a choice in how you look after yourself and come to terms with the termination.

WORRIES ABOUT HIV AND AIDS

If you are at all concerned about HIV and AIDS then it is possible that your pregnancy will bring these worries to the fore. You could start to panic about your past sex life or your current partner, especially if you know little about his sexual past. You may feel very frightened by the subject or confused by the information you have heard. You could be debating whether to have an HIV test or you may prefer not to know. You may already know you are HIV positive and be trying to reach a decision about your pregnancy in the light of this.

If you are feeling any of the above, the first thing that you will need is clear information. It is not within the scope of this book to address all the issues concerning women and AIDS but there are helplines and supportive organizations you can contact if you need more detailed information and advice (see Help and Information, p. 174).

If you have decided to have a termination, you may have enough to deal with right now, without getting terribly anxious about your sexual past. You can protect yourself and your partners in the future by having safer sex (see Chapter Nine, 'Contraception'). If you are considering an HIV test, it may be better to postpone your decision until you have had the abortion. You could double your anxiety if you try to cope with both things at the same time.

If you decide to continue with the pregnancy and feel you could have been at risk then you may want to have an HIV test to know where you stand. You should not feel under any obligation to take the test. You may decide that it is unlikely you have come into contact with the virus. You may feel that the test will cause you too much anxiety. If you are unsure about what to do you could ring a confidential helpline or discuss the pros and cons with a counsellor at a STD clinic. They will not pressurize you one way or another.

THE TEST

If you decide to have an HIV test, the best place to go is your local STD, GUM or special clinic. Most are attached to major hospitals and the National AIDS Helpline will give you the telephone number of the one nearest to you. The test is free at a STD clinic; it is also completely confidential. (The test will not be completely confidential if you go through your GP.) The clinic should also offer pre-and post-test counselling.

You should only have an HIV test if you are clear that you want the information and that you can cope with the result. Some women talk about having the test for peace of mind. It may certainly put your mind at rest if the result is negative, but it is important to consider the possibility of a positive result, too.

No one should pressurize you to have an HIV test without your consent. Some hospitals run anonymous testing programmes.

This is to get a better idea of the prevalence of HIV among the population. Your blood sample would not have your name on it so there is no way of tracing it back to you. If you are unsure whether the test is definitely anonymous or you find that doctors are 'encouraging' you to have the test, ring a helpline or talk to a health advisor at a Special Clinic in confidence, before giving your consent.

BEING HIV POSITIVE AND PREGNANT

If you are HIV positive and trying to decide whether to continue with the pregnancy it will be important that you have access to clear, unbiased information and non-judgemental counselling. In the past there has been a lot of pressure for women who know they are HIV positive to have abortions. You may still be advised against continuing the pregnancy but you have the right to make up your own mind.

As research and studies continue to be done around HIV infection in pregnancy, our understanding has changed and will continue to change. You should also contact specialist groups to discuss any other findings which may alter the picture.

In the past it was believed that continuing the pregnancy could be detrimental to your health. If you have symptoms or you are very unwell, then this could be the case. However, evidence suggests that, if you are well, your health will not be affected by the pregnancy. Although you should bear in mind that looking after a baby can be exhausting, and you should try to take positive steps to minimize the added stress.

There may also be a higher risk of your child being infected if you are symptomatic. HIV can be passed on to the child in the womb but statistics have changed regarding the probability of this happening. Some years ago it was believed to be about a 1 in 4 chance. More recent studies done in Europe have put the probability much lower – at 15 per cent or roughly a 1 in 7 chance.

Children born to HIV positive mothers carry their antibodies and therefore would test antibody positive for between 12 and 18 months. This means you may have to wait some time to find out if your child has been infected. There are other tests to measure the virus itself and immune function, which can establish the HIV status of a child younger than 18 months. However, these tests are more complicated and may not be performed outside the 'centres of excellence'. (In London – Great Ormond Street and St Mary's Paddington.) Children who are HIV positive may remain well for some time or may develop serious symptoms at an early stage. There is a possibility of HIV infection being passed on through breastfeeding and you may be advised not to breastfeed your child.

Like anyone else, you will be reaching your decision by weighing up the practical issues and your feelings about being a mother. In addition, you will have to face up to the possibility of your child being infected, and how you feel about the chances of this happening. You may also want to consider how much support is available for you and your child, should you get ill in the future. Living with such uncertainty can cause a great deal of stress, and you should try to find ways of minimizing this and making sure you prioritize your own emotional and physical well-being.

You may have to face a large amount of prejudice and disapproval if you decide to continue the pregnancy. While the majority of women are actively encouraged to have children, women who are HIV positive or disabled are frequently considered selfish or irresponsible for deciding to be mothers. This can be an added burden for you in trying to make the right decision. You could feel very isolated and worried about the reactions of others. You may feel angry at people's ignorance and prejudice but concerned at how this will affect your child's future. You may doubt your ability to cope with the difficulties ahead.

This is not to say that you are bound to face these problems. It will be important for you to consider the positive aspects of continuing the pregnancy as well. If you are asymptomatic, you could remain well for many years. You may already have access to good support and a caring partner or friends. If you have come to terms with your antibody status you may be very clear about what is important in your life and what you have to offer a child. You could feel confident in challenging discrimination and determined not to take on board other people's prejudiced attitudes.

Whatever you decide, it is crucial that you have support. Positively Women is an organization which offers a range of services to women with HIV infection. They will offer non-judgemental counselling to help you reach a decision, and will also offer advice and practical support if you choose to have the baby. You may find it very helpful to talk to other women who are antibody positive and have chosen to be mothers.

It is important not to feel a failure if you decide you cannot cope with being pregnant. If you have chosen a termination because of your HIV status, this may be a painful decision. You could find that the grief associated with the abortion will tap into a wider grief about being HIV positive, and sadness over lost opportunities. It will be a time when you will need to look after yourself and allow yourself to come to terms with your decision in your own way. Try and get as much support as you can, from those who are close to you and from your local Body Positive Group or Positively Women (see Help and Information, p. 174).

PREGNANCY AS A RESULT OF RAPE

Finding out that you are pregnant as a result of rape or sexual abuse can be devastating. It is something that you might have been dreading since the rape or abuse happened. It could be an enormous burden having to deal with the pregnancy as well as your feelings about the rape.

Whether you have been raped by a stranger or by someone you know, you could be feeling distraught, angry, frightened or powerless. You may find it hard to believe that this has actually happened to you. You might find it painful even to talk about or to know that it has had a profound effect on your life and how you feel about yourself. You could be coping with a court case, or the reactions of people close to you, or you may have decided not to tell anyone.

If you are able to tell the people close to you, can they offer you the support you need? Even if they are very supportive, it could be useful to contact a Rape Crisis Line or Victim Support Scheme, if you haven't done so already. You will be able to talk to another woman about your feelings, and will be offered support and counselling in the future (see Help and Information, p. 174).

You might find the decision about your pregnancy very clear. Many (but not all) woman feel strongly that having the child would be a constant reminder of their attacker and would not hesitate in choosing a termination. This could put you in a difficult position if you are anti-abortion or if you have other reasons for wanting to continue the pregnancy. You would need to think carefully about the reality of having a child in these circumstances. How would you cope in the future? What implications would there be for your relationship with the child and how you feel about yourself? Are you continuing the pregnancy in order to punish yourself for the rape? What would be the reactions of other people in your life?

If you do want to go ahead with the pregnancy, it will be essential you have people you can talk to and who will support you. If you cannot face having a termination, adoption might be a positive alternative for you (see Chapter Eight, 'Adoption and Fostering'). Throughout this book we have emphasized the importance of making the decision about your pregnancy on your own terms. If you have been raped it is particularly important that the decision is in your hands.

If you are ambivalent or confused, make sure that you have access to sympathetic and non-judgemental counselling. Even if you are clear you want an abortion, this does not mean it will be an easy time for you. You might find it very daunting having to tell strangers about the circumstances of the pregnancy. You may be feeling out of control and find the process of getting an abortion very traumatic.

You will need to look after yourself as much as possible. If you can, take someone you trust with you to the hospital or clinic. Hopefully, you will be treated with sensitivity and respect by doctors and other healthcare workers. You might need to take some time to come to terms with the rape and the abortion. Counselling should be available to you whenever you want it.

Sometimes it takes a while to be able to explore your feelings fully. Don't rush yourself. You might be anxious to 'get back to normal' and to forget what happened. Try not to dismiss or to trivialize your feelings. Recovering from the experience of rape will involve regaining a sense of control over your body as well as your life. Making the decision about your pregnancy on your own terms could help you to regain that sense of control. You had no choice about the rape, but you do have a choice about the future.

FOETAL ABNORMALITY

At least 2,000 parents each year undergo the traumatic experience of terminating a wanted pregnancy where the foetus is found to have a disability. More parents are likely to face this distressing dilemma as prenatal diagnosis becomes even more sophisticated. If you are in this position, you need advice and support to help you make an informed choice. Your obstetrician can give you specialized medical advice, and sympathetic understanding is available from SATFA (Support After Termination for Foetal Abnormality) (see Help and Information, p. 174).

FINDING OUT THAT SOMETHING IS WRONG

There are a number of tests which detect foetal abnormality, and you may be offered one or more of them depending on your age and medical history. They are not routinely offered to all pregnant women, partly because of the cost, partly because the small risk of miscarriage will in some cases outweigh the risk of abnormality.

Ultrasound Scanning is used for most pregnancies, regardless of suspected abnormalities. It passes harmless sound waves through your body which give a picture of the baby on screen. This may reveal abnormalities such as spina bifida.

Blood test for levels of alphafetoprotein (AFP) can indicate the need for further testing to confirm abnormality, and is usually carried out at about 17 weeks' gestation.

Chorionic Villus Sampling is usually performed between 8 to 12 weeks' gestation. It detects hereditary traits such as muscular dystrophy, thalassaemia, sickle-cell anaemia and haemophilia. CVS is performed by examining small pieces of placental tissue, and so carries a small risk of causing miscarriage.

Amniocentesis can detect Down's Syndrome. It is carried out between 16 to 19 weeks' gestation, and results usually take four weeks. The test is performed by inserting a needle into your abdomen and drawing off some fluid from the womb. This is then sent to a laboratory where it is cultured and examined. Amniocentesis carries a small risk of miscarriage.

Fetoscopy examines the foetus through a tiny fibre optic tube passed into the womb. This is performed between 16 to 18 weeks' gestation, and carries a small risk of miscarriage.

Waiting for the results of these tests is a very stressful experience, particularly as you are likely to be well advanced in pregnancy. At this stage you may have built up a relationship with your foetus, and an expectancy of producing a living baby.

A bad result can be devastating, like a full-scale bereavement. Pregnancy is a time when women start adjusting to their future life by projecting a personality on to the foetus, and forming a relationship with their future child. Discovering that there is a problem with your pregnancy can be a tremendous shock which totally disrupts that precious and new relationship. Even if the pregnancy is not terminated, you have in effect lost the child you were expecting, and the future you had planned.

As well as your fear and distress, you may feel considerable guilt and anger – with yourself, your partner, or your doctor. At the same time, you will be facing intense pressure to decide whether to continue your pregnancy – and this decision will usually have to be made within a few days. Some women know immediately what they need to do. You may even feel that you have no real choice: maybe you feel the extent of disability is so severe as to be incompatible with life, or maybe you believe abortion is totally wrong. Alternatively, you may be unsure of what to do, and making this decision could turn out to be one of the most difficult tasks you will ever have to face.

MAKING YOUR CHOICE

It is very important that you arm yourself with the fullest possible information to help you work out what is best for the future welfare of yourself and your family. You will need to consider:

- **the child's potential quality of life;**
- **the effects on your own life and career;**
- **the effect on your family;**
- **your physical capacity to provide the care needed.**

It may be helpful to write down the questions you would like to ask your doctor and other specialists. It can also help to talk to other families who have faced your dilemma: both those who have opted for termination, and those who have raised a child affected with the abnormality threatening your pregnancy.

You may find yourself under tremendous pressure from your doctor and others to opt for abortion. Our society devalues people with disabilities, preferring them to be kept out of sight and out of mind – or preferably not existing at all. Women are given little practical help or encouragement to bring up disabled children. This prejudice is so strong that the prospect of giving birth to a disabled child can seem very frightening. Yet many people don't appreciate the wide range of potential covered by the diagnosis of 'disability': with appropriate medical help and modern teaching aids, your child may enjoy a high quality of life. You may find it easier to get a balanced picture by meeting other families in your position, and children with similar disabilities. Then you can see for yourself your child's potential quality of life and capacity for human relationships – and you can assess your own resources and ability to provide suitable practical care for that child.

On the other hand, our society also expects women to sacrifice their lives to motherhood, and – depending on the severity of the abnormality and the practical help available to you – you could be being called upon to do just that. Your wider family and friends may put you under unfair pressure to continue the pregnancy – and brand you as 'selfish' or 'heartless' if you do not. Down's Syndrome children are often depicted as particularly affectionate and endearing, and living with this disability is sometimes senti-mentalized beyond all recognition. Choosing abortion does not necessarily mean your maternal feelings are lacking; the foetus is not the only person to be considered here. Caring for a child with a disability can have a devastating effect on your life, with huge repercussions for your partner and existing or future children as well. It may be that your most loving and responsible course of action – for the physical and emotional wellbeing of *everyone* involved – is abortion. It could be, of course, that the abnormality is so severe that termination can only be considered a kindness. But that is a choice only you can make.

CONTINUING THE PREGNANCY

Choosing to continue a pregnancy with a high risk of abnormality can magnify all the normal hopes and fears of pregnancy: what will the baby look like? How will it affect your relationship with your partner? How will you cope? Once the baby is born, you may feel isolated, patronized or judged by others. You may not even *like* your child at first (a very common experience but no less guilt-inducing for that); you may wonder in despair if you have made the right choice.

These feelings are common to many new mothers, but will be compounded by the very real difficulties faced by parents of handicapped children. It is *not* easy to raise a disabled child: it can be lonely, exhausting, and seemingly never-ending. But disabilities cover a very wide continuum of physical and mental challenge, and often our fear and dislike of human difference can obscure the rewards and potentials of this task.

You can start preparing yourself before the birth, for example, in the following ways:

- **Medical support** from your GP, obstetrician and paediatrician. You may need extra medical help in pregnancy and labour. You will certainly need lots of information about your child's disability, and its future prognosis.
- **Practical help and welfare benefits** available to you from your local social services and Citizens Advice Bureau. Make sure you put in any claims in good time. It will help if you can organize practical help from your friends and family as well – not only does this save you from total exhaustion, it is also good for your baby not to be socially isolated.
- **Emotional support** from the many organizations that can help you through your pregnancy and beyond (see Help & Information, p. 174). Some of these are self-help groups where you can get together and exchange information with other parents in your situation. Others can offer you counselling, parenting workshops, and practical help.

CHOOSING TERMINATION

Terminations on the grounds of foetal abnormality will usually be done by medical induction (see Methods of Abortion, p. 97 in Chapter Five). This means that you will be conscious throughout most of the abortion experience, and it is a good idea to plan how you want to deal with that.

You may be given a private room, but it is more likely that you will be on a gynaecological or labour ward next to women who cannot have babies or who are giving birth to healthy children, which can compound everyone's distress. You may be offered painkillers and/or sedatives. Labour will usually last 6–24 hours, so think carefully whether you want to be helped through by drugs (see p. 97) or whether you prefer to 'live' the experience, and maybe come to terms with it quicker. This decision may be affected by whether you are allowed to have a partner or a friend with you. Ask the hospital, then consider whether you would find companionship unhelpful, or whether you would rather not have to deal with their distress.

Your decision will also be affected by whether you want to see and hold your baby after birth. Many parents do want to do this, and the hospital will usually be sympathetic to this request. Seeing and holding your baby – complete with abnormality – can really help you to come to terms with the choice you have made, or the love you have lost. If, on the other hand, you do not want to see the baby, don't feel ashamed not doing so. Everyone has their own way of grieving. The hospital will usually take a photo of your baby at birth, in case you change your mind later.

AFTERWARDS

There are no legal requirements to bury or cremate a baby born dead before 24 weeks: they are usually cremated after post-mortem. But hospitals will usually be sympathetic to requests for a proper burial service. Alternatively, you could arrange your own memorial service or ritual in whatever way suits you best.

Going home after the termination can be very distressing. Friends and colleagues may not have heard and will ring up to ask you about the baby; your breasts may be producing milk; you may be suffering from post-natal depression in addition to your bereavement. You may feel a range of emotions including guilt, rage at your partner, envy of other mothers, and emptiness.

Well-meaning friends can cause a lot of upset by trivializing your grief or suggesting you replace your lost baby as soon as possible with another one. You should not rush into another pregnancy straight away: your body and your relationship need time to recover while you go through the grieving process. You may also need specialist medical advice and/or genetic counselling before trying again.

CHAPTER FIVE

CHOOSING ABORTION

One in three women in this country will at some point in their lives terminate an unwanted pregnancy. Although abortion has only been legal since 1967 (and then only in certain circumstances) it has been used throughout history to help women limit the size of their families. Recipes that brought on miscarriage were known and used in ancient China, India, Egypt, Greece and Rome – and openly sold in chemists' shops right up into this century.

Folk wisdom has always differentiated between early abortion (thought of as 'bringing down' one's period, or 'making oneself regular') and abortion after 'quickening', when the foetus can be felt moving (at around 18 weeks' gestation). English common law reflected this distinction, as did early Christianity, which allowed abortion up to the time when the foetus acquired a soul (thought to be at 40 days for a male foetus and 80 days for a female!).

Criminalization of abortion formed part of the early medical profession's attempt to wrest control of gynaecological practice away from lay healers. Abortion was made illegal in the middle of the nineteenth century, with penalties of up to life imprisonment for both the pregnant woman and the abortionist. This did not stop an estimated 100,000 women each year going to illegal back-street abortionists.

In the 1930s Dr Alec Bourne performed an abortion on a 14-year-old-girl who had been gang-raped by soldiers. He then gave himself up to the police, and in the important trial that followed the judge ruled that doctors could perform abortion where any serious impairment of physical or mental health might endanger the woman's life. This ruling led to a situation in which middle-class women paid Harley Street doctors to certify them unfit to continue a pregnancy, while poor women continued to frequent backstreet abortionists. Not only was this unfair, it also resulted in hundreds of women being injured or killed each year by dangerous illegal abortions. Public and medical concern, combined with the campaigning efforts of the Abortion Law Reform Association, led to the passing of the 1967 Abortion Act.

THE PRESENT LAW

The 1967 Act, as amended by the Human Fertilization and Embryology Act 1990, allows abortion:

> *where two doctors certify that they are 'of the opinion formed in good faith' that an abortion is necessary on one or more of the following grounds:*
>
> 1 *Your life would be at risk if you continued with the pregnancy.*
>
> 2 *Continuing the pregnancy would mean 'more of a risk to your physical or mental health than if it were terminated'.*
> [As continuing a pregnancy is nearly always more dangerous than abortion, this clause allows sympathetic doctors to authorize termination – and indeed the vast majority of abortions are performed on these grounds. They must, however, relate their decision to your individual circumstances, not to an average risk factor.]
>
> 3 *Your pregnancy would damage the physical and mental health of your existing child or children.*
>
> 4 *There is a substantial risk that the child would be born with a serious handicap.*

Under these grounds abortion is allowed up until the 24th week of pregnancy, but there is no time limit where the mother's health is seriously at risk of permanent grave damage or where the foetus is substantially handicapped.

77

Your social situation, feelings, housing, state of relationship and so on are not in themselves grounds for abortion, but the doctors can take these factors into account when calculating the effect of this pregnancy on your physical and emotional well-being. In practice, this law puts a lot of power into the hands of doctors: some will go by your wishes, believing that forcing a women to continue an unwanted pregnancy must be harmful to her well-being. Others will require evidence of serious problems such as ill health or severe poverty.

HOW TO GET AN ABORTION

If you want an abortion *you should seek help quickly*. Late abortion is more risky and more upsetting than early termination: it can also be very difficult to get NHS (i.e. free) treatment after 12 weeks of pregnancy, and private abortion fees rise steeply after this time. Even if you are not sure that abortion is the right choice for you, it is worth seeking help straight away: you can go ahead with the practical arrangements while you are receiving counselling help and thinking through your options – and you can cancel the operation at any time.

GETTING AN NHS ABORTION

If you want a free NHS abortion you will normally need to ask your GP to refer you to a gynaecologist. Alternatively, you can go through a Family Planning Clinic or Brook Advisory Centre.

YOUR GP

Your GP has a legal duty to provide you with confidential advice and appropriate referral, but they do not have to approve abortion, and in practice their attitudes and actions will vary widely.

Ideally, your GP will be sympathetic and refer you to the local hospital for further treatment. They may authorize abortion (sign the 'blue form') to help speed up your treatment. Alternatively, you may be told that you will not be able to get NHS termination because of local policy, waiting lists, or your stage of pregnancy. If so, ask to be referred to a pregnancy advisory clinic.

Your GP may decide that you are not legally eligible for abortion. Remember that this is their opinion, and that you may still be able to find another doctor willing to help you, either within the same practice or at another surgery altogether.

YOUR FAMILY PLANNING CLINIC

If you regularly attend a Family Planning Clinic, they can help you – just ring and make an immediate appointment. If you are not a client already, they may not be able to see you, but you could try explaining to the clinic staff that you need urgent counselling about a termination and they may be able to refer you for help.

As with your GP, the FPC may be able to refer you for an NHS abortion, or they may suggest you attend a local charity or private clinic.

BROOK ADVISORY CENTRES

If you are under 26, your local Brook Advisory Centre can give you pregnancy testing, counselling and abortion referral. This will be for an NHS termination if possible, otherwise to a charitable clinic.

THE NON-NHS ALTERNATIVE

Nearly half of all women seeking abortion help in this country are treated in the private sector: some so that they can get their abortion more quickly and in a sympathetic atmosphere, but most who have been denied NHS help because of waiting lists, lack of resources or unsympathetic consultants. If this happens to you, seek help quickly. **Do not wait to make an appointment until you can afford the operation** – you can go ahead with making arrangements while you raise the money, and you should be aware that abortion becomes more expensive the longer you leave it. Charity clinics will often help you if you are in financial difficulty: either by helping you identify sources of funding, or by arranging a staggered payment of fees, or even by giving you a partial or total grant to cover the cost of your treatment. If you can't afford the fees, tell the staff when you book your appointment, and ask for a confidential interview to discuss the problem.

CHARITY CLINICS

If you choose to attend a charitable pregnancy advisory bureau you can contact them yourself, without needing to see your GP first. The British Pregnancy Advisory Service and Marie Stopes Clinics offer abortion advice and help including pregnancy testing, non-directive counselling, termination of pregnancy (where appropriate) and post-abortion counselling. They are approved by the Department of Health, have been established for over 25 years and are motivated by the wish to help women in your position – so all will be sympathetic and understanding. Waiting times for appointments are usually short and the operation can be arranged within a few days.

The British Pregnancy Advisory Service is the largest provider with some twenty-six branches and seven nursing homes across the country. Marie Stopes has branches in London, Leeds and Manchester. They all charge fees on a non-profit-making basis, usually starting at around £250 to cover counselling, consultation, surgery and post-abortion care. The cost of a late abortion can be as much as £600, but all the charities offer help to women in financial hardship.

PRIVATE (COMMERCIAL) CLINICS

A number of private clinics are also licensed by the Department of Health to perform abortions, and some have their own pregnancy advisory bureaux where you can see two doctors to approve your termination. These clinics can usually be found in the phone book or advertised in women's magazines. They are closely monitored by the Department of Health, so clinical standards are up to scratch, but the counselling may be offered by a doctor or nurse rather than a trained professional.

It is worth ringing round to compare prices and facilities before committing yourself to a particular clinic.

A PRIVATE GYNAECOLOGIST

Your GP may offer to refer you to a private gynaecologist, or the gynaecologist at the hospital may offer to treat you privately if there are long waiting lists for NHS care. Be aware that the prices charged for private treatment may be very high, while the standard of care is usually no higher than that in a charity clinic.

AGENCY ARRANGEMENTS

Instead of or as well as providing abortions in their own hospitals, some health authorities make contractual arrangements with non-NHS services. This means that you may end up having an abortion in a private or charitable nursing home at the expense of the NHS. In many ways this is an ideal arrangement: you should get first-rate medical and counselling care, quickly and for free.

EXTRA-CONTRACTUAL REFERRALS

Another way of obtaining NHS funding for a non-NHS abortion is by an Extra-Contractual Referral, or ECR. ECRs are made where a GP agrees that a woman is entitled to an NHS abortion, but for some reason the NHS is not able to carry out treatment (long waiting lists, for example). They can then make a one-off arrangement, costs of which will be met from the budget which funds contractual abortion services. Charity abortion clinics will try to arrange an ECR if they think you are eligible, or you could try asking your GP if you think you are eligible. You will need to provide proof that you live within the health authority area, and that you meet the relevant criteria. Only a small minority of abortions are currently paid for by this method.

WHAT HAPPENS NEXT

Whether you go to the NHS, a charity clinic, or the private sector, the procedure you undergo will be broadly similar.

1. **Confirmation of pregnancy.** Even if you have done your own pregnancy test, this will usually be confirmed with another urine test.
2. **Seeing the first doctor.** This could be your GP, a private gynaecologist or a clinic doctor. They will confirm pregnancy with an internal examination and ask you some questions about your social situation and your medical history, including any previous pregnancies. You will be asked why you want an abortion, and whether you have considered the alternative options. If they agree that abortion is appropriate, they will sign the 'blue form' (HSA1) and take your blood pressure. They will also need to take blood to test for anaemia and to check your blood group. You may need to have an ultrasound scan if you are late in pregnancy or if there is some doubt about the gestation.
3. **The second doctor.** If you are at a charity or private clinic, you will see the second doctor immediately. If you are having treatment on the NHS, you will probably be referred to hospital. Although this doctor will have your notes, they will want to confirm that you are making an informed choice for abortion. If they agree, they will sign the 'blue form' and you can make an appointment for the operation. If they don't sign, go back to your first doctor **immediately.**
4. **Counselling.** You must be offered counselling, by law, but the quality of this varies widely. BPAS, for example, employs trained counsellors (all women) who will be sympathetic and allow you to decide exactly how much or how little discussion

you want. This service is valuable but it may cost you extra.

5. **Appointment for termination.** Once two doctors have approved your abortion, you will be booked in for the operation as soon as possible.

You may be offered 'daycare' treatment, which means you will be discharged after about four hours. If you are having a non-NHS operation you will need to:

- **Be under 14 weeks pregnant.**
- **Live within two hours' travelling distance from the hospital or nursing home.**
- **Have a GP who can provide emergency cover – they will be informed of the date of the operation before it takes place.**

You will also be advised to have someone to collect you and take you home, although this is not compulsory. If you cannot meet the daycare criteria, you will need to stay in overnight.

If you are having NHS treatment you will be referred to a hospital, either to a specialist unit or a mixed ward. The specialist units are usually very good, but in some areas you may have to go on a general gynaecological ward. This can be distressing, and you may have to face a certain amount of hostility from other patients (and possibly even from staff).

The charities and specialist commercial clinics will refer you to a nursing home where you will be in a small ward or room with other women in the same position as yourself, and where the staff are likely to be sympathetic and understanding. All these nursing homes are maintained by the Department of Health and the clinical standards are excellent.

NEGOTIATING THE SYSTEM

If you have made your decision, then you will probably want the operation as quickly as possible. It is usually possible to arrange for a non-NHS abortion within a few days, but NHS treatment can take much longer – four to six weeks is not uncommon. Hanging on for weeks, not knowing if the hospital will agree to a termination, can be agonizing. You could be dealing with bureaucracy and struggling to get access to services when you are feeling particularly anxious and distressed.

You may need to be persistent and assertive to get what you want. You might find that it is impossible to get your termination on the NHS and be forced to go privately. You could be sympathetically treated or find you have to deal with patronizing or abusive behaviour from those who should be helping you.

You deserve to be treated with respect. You should be clear about who is prepared to help you and who is not. You will need to know early on whether the NHS can offer you a bed or whether they are wasting your time. You have the right to information, and answers to your questions. If you feel you're going to be intimidated, take an ally with you. This could be your partner, a close friend, a family member, or a sympathetic social worker.

How you are treated and your experience of the operation is likely to affect how you will feel later. It is important, therefore, to try and establish some control over what is happening to you rather than feel that you are at the mercy of doctors' whims or mindless bureaucracy.

CHOOSING TO GO PRIVATELY

If you do go privately, you are likely to get a termination without much delay, and unlikely to have to justify being a 'deserving case'. However, you will have to find the money for the operation. This could involve having to tell other people in your life, in order to ask for help.

The charity organizations do offer financial assistance but this will involve disclosing detailed information about your personal and financial situation. Because their resources are limited, and there are lots of women who need help, they may want you to exhaust all other options before agreeing to a loan or grant.

Some women have commented that having an abortion in the private sector can feel as through you are on a conveyor belt. You may find it disturbing to see the abortion in terms of a cash transaction. The charities are all non-profit-making and committed to providing a good service. Many women would accept packed waiting rooms and a certain amount of being hurried through the system as the price of not having to wait for weeks for the operation. You may even be able to go on a 'cancellations' list for an opportunity to take up a bed at short notice. However, make sure you are given enough time to discuss the operation and to sort out any difficulties.

Most of the staff at the charity clinics are women and they will have experience in putting you at ease and answering your questions. They will also be used to seeing women who are nervous of what to expect. If you are anxious about the internal examination it may be possible for you to see a woman doctor. It is a good idea to try and ask clearly for what you want, rather than waiting for someone to guess what you are worried about.

NEGOTIATING THE NHS

The quality of NHS abortion services vary widely. You may find that your GP is extremely helpful and that your local hospital offers you a good service. However, you have no legal right to a termination on the NHS. This means you could have to spend time proving that you need the abortion or protesting at long delays.

Most of us can be intimidated by doctors. Doctors usually have a lot more power than their patients and it can be very difficult to challenge their authority or even to ask for explanations. The abortion law adds to this power by putting the decision in the doctor's hands rather than yours. The law says that doctor knows best and, if the doctor agrees with this, they may see it as their right to question your decision, make judgements about you or simply refuse to help you.

The abortion law gives doctors an ideal opportunity to play God. Despite this, some GPs and consultants will be sympathetic and will respect your wishes. Others may be unhelpful or patronizing. If you do encounter this sort of behaviour, it may be deeply satisfying to walk out of the room or hit the doctor over the head with a stethoscope. Unfortunately, this is not going to get you what you want. It is possible to be very calm and polite, while making it clear that you expect the doctor to provide you with a service – not to offer you a lecture on your morals or tell you what a silly girl you've been.

It may not be easy to stand up for what you want, but in order to look after yourself and get the help you need it could be worth considering the following points:

- **Take time before the appointment to sort out in your own mind why you want the abortion.** Be prepared to explain your reasons calmly and unapologetically. If this is daunting, write them down first or go over them with a friend.
- **Compile a list of questions you want answers to.** Take the list with you. Some doctors are not very good at answering patients' questions, so be insistent if you need to be. If the consultant has agreed to the operation, you have the right to know which method will be used and anything else you feel is relevant. If you don't get a straight answer, then ask if there is anyone else who can help you.
- **Try to establish early on in the consultation whether this person is prepared to help you or not.** This means you will not be wasting time fighting a losing battle. You may be able to see someone else or decide to go privately.
- **Try not to feel undermined if your doctor is patronizing or hostile.** Don't get aggressive or too upset, but don't let yourself be intimidated either.

- **Be assertive.** For instance.

    Doctor: *You're a healthy young woman. I think you'll probably want to keep the baby if you think it over. I mean, there's no real reason, is there, why you can't have a child, hmm? You've got a boyfriend, somewhere to live. Think it over.*

    You: *I have already spent some time thinking and talking about my decision. I'm now really sure I want an abortion. I've explained my reasons to you and, although you may not approve of them, they are good enough for me. What I want to know is can you help me get a termination on the NHS?*

One of the techniques of being assertive is called the 'broken record'. This involves calmly repeating your request until you get an answer that you are satisfied with. It stops the other person fobbing you off with excuses or diverting you with irrelevant arguments. Basically, you want to know if you can get a termination and how soon it will be. You need to keep coming back to this point until you get a straight answer:

    Doctor: *Why don't you think about it and come and see me in a couple of days?*

    You: *I have thought about it and and I've made my decision. What I really need to know is, can you help me or do I need to go elsewhere?*

    Doctor: *It won't be easy, you know, getting you an appointment at the hospital. Why don't you give me a ring in a week? That will give you some more time to think it over.*

    You: *I know that I want an abortion. I want one as soon as possible. Is there any reason why you can't make an appointment for me now?*

    Doctor: *Well, if you're really sure, I suppose I could try ringing them now.*

- **Make sure you are clear about the information you're given.** If you are given an appointment at the hospital, check that you know where to go. Be clear about who it is you are going to see and what the purpose of the consultation is. Some women have waited weeks for an appointment which they assume is to arrange their operation, only to find it is another lengthy assessment by a social worker or a consultant.

- **Take someone with you for moral support.** You may just want them to hold your hand in the waiting room, but if you feel unconfident, ask if they may come and see the doctor with you. It can be easier to be assertive when you have someone else to back you up.

You might find it difficult to challenge patronizing or arrogant attitudes, knowing that the doctor can ultimately choose whether to grant or withhold the termination. However, if you make it clear that you deserve to be treated with respect, it will be harder for professionals you encounter to bully or dismiss you.

Don't feel as though it's your fault if you cannot get a termination or if you are treated badly. However assertive you are, you won't be able to change entrenched attitudes – and your Health Authority may just have inadequate facilities for abortions. If you are angry at the way you have been treated then it may be worth making a complaint once you have had the termination. This might help you feel less powerless, and could make a difference in how women are treated in the future. Write down everything that happened and what was said to you, so it will stay clear in your mind. If you want to complain about your GP you should contact the Family Health Services Authority or the Community Health Council. Complaints about NHS hospitals should be sent to the hospital or to the Community Health Council. If you want to complain about a non-NHS clinic you could write to the manager of the clinic or contact the Department of Health.

RACISM IN THE SYSTEM

If you are a black woman living in Britain, racist attitudes will probably not come as a surprise and you will have already developed techniques for dealing with them. However, you may want to think of ways of protecting yourself while ensuring that you get the best service you can.

If you are faced with doctors and other professionals who have racist attitudes, this is not going to make it easy for you to feel positive about your decision. Racism cuts many ways, so this does not necessarily mean you will have less access to abortion services (although it might). If you are black or Asian it may be assumed that having children is more important than your career plans – without actually hearing whether or not this is true for you. If you are Afro-Caribbean it could be assumed that you will choose single parenthood rather than abortion. You may find yourself patronized by doctors who believe you are not capable of using contraception correctly.

You might find that people's ignorance of your culture or beliefs prevents them from appreciating your reasons for wanting a termination or the doubts and anxieties you have about it. Instead of being an individual with your own set of problems and circumstances, you could be seen as representative of your race or culture. If abortion is disapproved of in your culture, you could feel that you are somehow letting the side down.

Of course, you are not going to be able to take on and change the system in the process of getting your abortion. The important thing is to concentrate on getting the best service you can and, if possible, refuse to tolerate unacceptable behaviour. How much you are able to do this is up to you. It takes a lot of courage to challenge racist behaviour. As we have said earlier (see p. 88), it may be easier to make a formal complaint at a later date than to confront the person there and then.

Explain clearly what your needs are. It might be useful to take a friend with you to the hospital or to contact a community organization for support. It will be very important to have support if you are being pressurized into accepting a sterilization or 'persuaded' to use a certain form of contraception. You should be given the freedom to make your own contraceptive choices and not be bullied by the doctor into agreeing to anything you don't feel comfortable with.

REPEAT ABORTION

More than 1 in 10 abortions are performed on women who have already had at least one termination. This fact shocks many people: 'I'm not anti-abortion,' they say, 'but it shouldn't be used as a form of birth control.' It's as if everyone is entitled to just one mistake, after which they get branded as irresponsible. Indeed, many hospitals have a policy to allow women 'one abortion each', after which they are turned away to the private sector.

In reality, women **can** 'get unlucky' twice. All methods of contraception can fail, and most women will face an unplanned pregnancy at least once in their lives.

The physical risks of repeated abortions are not as high as you may fear, though they increase with the length of pregnancy. Early abortion is very safe, and the risk does not appear to be cumulative. In other words, providing each abortion goes without a hitch, you will be at no higher risk than someone who has never had a previous abortion.

However low the physical risk, having another abortion may make you feel very bad about yourself. You could also be worried that you will be told off, or even refused help, by the doctor from whom you will be seeking an abortion. When you go, you will be asked about your past pregnancies and abortions as part of the medical examination. Many women feel very reluctant to disclose previous terminations in case it jeopardizes their chances of getting another one; indeed, some doctors do see repeat abortions as some kind of personal insult, and may treat you accordingly. Nevertheless, it is a good idea to be open about your medical history, for two reasons: first, that it may be relevant to your current medical treatment and, second, that it will be more difficult for you to address any anxiety and grief you feel about **this** abortion if you are not able to discuss the previous one.

The counsellor will be used to seeing women who have had repeated abortions, and she shouldn't be shocked or disapproving (if she is, she's not doing her job properly). She will offer you help to explore your feelings and concerns about both abortions: it will probably be worthwhile to take up this offer, as it allows you to work through your painful feelings without being judged.

Abortion **can** be an easier experience the second time around, because you know what to expect or because you are older and more in control of your life. But you might also find a second abortion very difficult if your previous experience was a bad one. If you were very frightened, unsupported or badly treated at the hospital, you are more likely to feel anxious and defensive this time around.

It is important to discuss these feelings: a second abortion can revive painful memories and unresolved distress for many women. These feelings may interfere with your ability to make an informed choice about *this* pregnancy, unless you can acknowledge and deal with them.

Of course, your previous experience can also be turned to your advantage if you can learn from it. Look at what made your last abortion a difficult experience, and what you could do to help yourself this time. Would you have felt better if you had had more counselling, or more information, or a friend to stay the night?

If you do become pregnant again, it might simply be bad luck: some women are just very fertile, or cannot find a form of contraception to suit them. And whether or not there is some hidden reason, there is no need for you to feel guilty or silly. Prevention **is** better than cure, however, and it is worth looking back over what happened to see if this experience can teach you something for the future.

Some women become pregnant repeatedly as an expression of unresolved conflicts. You may be able to recognize something of yourself in the following:

- Do you enjoy the status of pregnancy, or the high drama of unplanned pregnancy?
- Do you secretly want a baby?
- Is pregnancy the only way you can get care and attention from the people around you?
- Do you use contraception haphazardly, or not at all, as a

way of expressing unhappiness with your sexuality or with a particular relationship?

- Are repeated abortions a way of punishing yourself?
- Are repeated abortions a way of signalling feelings of hopelessness about your ability to change your current situation?
- Do you feel in control of your body and your sex life, or do you feel controlled by others?
- Do you respect your body – and yourself?
- Do you enjoy taking risks?

There is no need to punish yourself for these feelings: it is more constructive to talk them over with a friend or a counsellor, and to plan the changes you could make in the future. These might include making a positive commitment to contraception (see Chapter Nine, 'Contraception') or facing up to a desire to become a mother.

Maybe you promised yourself 'never again' after your last abortion, and now you feel like a hopeless failure. If the abortion was very recent, you may feel particularly humiliated at becoming pregnant again so quickly, and under extra pressure to justify your decision to have an abortion. Unfortunately, other people will sometimes back up these self-destructive thoughts.

It is very easy to adopt other people's attitudes and think badly of yourself because you need another abortion. Some women even deny themselves this option because they feel they don't 'deserve' it. If you feel this way, try reminding yourself that no child should ever be born in order to punish its mother: your future children 'deserve' to be loved and respected – and so do you.

IRISH WOMEN

The 1967 Abortion Act does not extend to Northern Ireland. While abortion is legally permissable in some restricted circumstances, the law is so confused that most doctors 'play safe' by refusing to perform abortions in almost every case short of saving a woman's life.

In the Republic of Ireland abortion is not only illegal but also unconstitutional. For some years it was forbidden even to pass on information about abortion services in Britain, and the legal system tried to stop women needing abortions from travelling to the UK. Times are changing, however, and a recent referendum showed strong public support for overturning this censorship, and allowing women the right to travel. The Government is now looking at legislation to enshrine these rights.

Abortion can be a particularly difficult experience for Irish women. Even if you do not have any religious or moral objections to abortion, it is hard not to feel affected by the secular taboo against premarital sexual activity, contraception and abortion. There are also a great number of practical difficulties to deal with: raising the travel fare as well as the operation fee; getting information on where to go and what to expect; coping with a different culture at what is already a bewildering and upsetting time; and explaining your absence to family and friends.

Finding out where to go for help, making practical arrangements and raising the money for your expenses can take a lot of time and effort – time that ideally you would be spending looking after yourself and thinking through your situation. It can be hard to make such an important decision in secrecy, without being able to discuss your options with family, friends or professional advisers. It is especially difficult to make an informed choice when it is so difficult to get accurate information. And it can be frightening to admit to yourself any doubts you may have about the abortion when you are in a state of panic about how you will get to England in time for a safe and inexpensive operation.

Counsellors in the charities which provide abortion services find that Irish women are particularly unlikely to know what is involved in abortion, and to have exaggerated fears about the health risks – hardly surprising when the information they need has been censored. It can be very difficult to help where a woman is ambivalent about the abortion – English women can go away for a couple of days to think through their decision and discuss it with family and friends, but it is not feasible for Irish women to make repeated trips back overseas. Once she has made the trip to England, it is not easy for an Irish woman to deal properly with any doubts that may surface: she may feel that, since she has risked so much to get this far, she has to go through with it.

WHERE TO GET HELP

If you live in Northern Ireland you can get confidential pregnancy counselling and information on abortion services from the Ulster Pregnancy Advisory Association or the Northern Ireland Family Planning Association. If you live in Eire you can get help and advice from the Dublin Well Woman Centre or the Irish Family Planning Association (see Help and Information, p. 174). They can refer you to Liverpool or London; you will usually need to meet the full cost of treatment plus travel and accommodation costs. If you can prove you have been resident in England for six weeks you may be able to get an NHS termination.

Even though abortion is illegal in Ireland, it is **not** a crime for you to have an abortion in England, which means you cannot be prosecuted back home after the act.

The abortion charities in London and Liverpool are used to helping Irish woman (about 5,000 each year), and it is a good idea to book an appointment with them before you travel to England. You will need to make arrangements to be away for 2 to 3 days, and you may find it helpful to contact one of the support groups which help Irish women seeking abortion in England which, in London, means the Irish Women's Abortion Support Group. In Liverpool, BPAS can put you in touch with Escort or the Liverpool Abortion Support Service. All these groups can offer you overnight accommodation and emotional support during your stay in England (see Help and Information, p. 174).

Once you have reached the clinic, you will be assessed for termination under the conditions of the 1967 Abortion Act. You will find the charity clinics very sympathetic to your situation, and they will usually be able to arrange for you to have the operation the next day.

AFTER ABORTION

Six weeks after the abortion, you will need to go for a medical check-up to make sure you don't have an infection: **this is not illegal and they will respect your confidentiality**. You can go to your own GP or Family Planning Clinic, or to the Dublin Well Woman Centre (see Help and Information, p. 174).

As important as your physical well-being is the care you take of your emotional welfare. Elsewhere in this book the variety of emotional reactions to abortion are explored and explained: Irish women, who have to cope with these feelings in an atmosphere of silence and fear, may have particular difficulty in coming to terms with their experience, and with social condemnation of the decision they have made. It really is worthwhile getting emotional support at this time: if you can't talk to your family or friends, get help from any of the organizations mentioned above or listed in Help and Information, p. 174. Undergoing abortion in a foreign country can be a very lonely experience – but hard though it might be to believe, other women in your neighbourhood have probably been through the same thing. You are not alone – so get all the support you need and deserve.

BEFORE THE OPERATION

Before you go in for your operation, try to arrange things so that you don't have too much stress to deal with either before or after the abortion. Arrange for someone to pick you up afterwards, and stay with you for a night. You will also need to arrange some time off work: if you are having an early abortion (up to 13 weeks), two days will normally be sufficient, but if you are having a later operation you might like to consider taking the whole week off.

If you are having daycare treatment, you may only be in

hospital for a few hours. Take with you some stick-on sanitary towels (not tampons), and any medicines, including inhalers, which have been prescribed by your doctor.

If you are staying in overnight, you will probably be sitting around a lot, so you should also pack some reading material, a nightdress, slippers, a dressing gown and toilet needs such as toothbrush, soap and towel.

Before any operation involving general anaesthetic, it is vital that you **do not smoke, eat or drink anything**, unless you have been instructed otherwise. This is because of the risk of vomiting while unconscious: if you have eaten, the operation will be delayed until your stomach is empty again. You will normally be told not to eat anything after the midnight before your operation: 'anything' includes cups of tea, sweets, chewing gum and even water. The only exception to this is prescribed medicines, which should be swallowed with as little water as you can manage.

If you have been told you are having your operation later on in the day, you will usually be allowed a light breakfast of tea and toast. If you are having medical induction, you will be advised to have a good breakfast: it may be some hours before you can eat again.

You will need to decide who you want to be told about the abortion, as the nursing staff are usually instructed not to give out information about clients without your express permission – not even to say if you are there.

When you arrive at the hospital or nursing home you will be asked for some registration details, including an emergency telephone number. If you are not receiving NHS treatment, you will usually then have to pay the operation fee in full. Be warned that some nursing homes will expect you to pay cash, though others accept credit cards.

Check beforehand if you are allowed visitors, and whether there is a phone you can use on the ward. If you are accompanied by a friend or partner they will have to wait in a lounge that may not have smoking or refreshment facilities. You will not be allowed to smoke on the ward, so find out if there is a smoking room available if you think this might cause difficulty.

METHODS OF ABORTION
RU486 (THE 'ABORTION PILL')

If you are at a very early stage in pregnancy (up to 9 weeks' gestation), between eighteen and thirty-five and not a heavy smoker, you may be offered a new form of medical abortion called RU486 or mifegyne.

RU486 is a steroid hormone which interrupts pregnancy by blocking the production of progesterone, the hormone which builds up the placenta to nourish the foetus. When used in conjunction with a substance called prostaglandin, which brings on contractions and opens up the cervix, RU486 has a success rate equivalent to that of surgical abortion.

If you have been offered a medical abortion with RU486, you will need to make three visits to a hospital or approved clinic. During the first, you will be given three RU486 tablets to swallow with a glass of water, and asked to wait for two hours before going home. You should not smoke or drink alcohol from this point until two days after your abortion is complete.

You must then wait forty-eight hours before returning to the clinic. You may start light bleeding and stomach cramps, as if you were having a period; you can take painkillers if you want, but avoid aspirin or ibuprofen. There is a very small chance that you will expel the pregnancy at home. This is not dangerous but you should ring the hospital as soon as possible if this happens. You might find this forty-eight hours a stressful time, so try to get lots of support and understanding from those around you.

Two days later you return to the hospital or clinic, where a doctor will insert a vaginal pessary (like a mini-tampon) containing prostaglandin. Prostaglandin helps the womb to push out its contents, and at this point you will start bleeding quite heavily and experiencing cramps. You may be in bed for some or all of this time. In effect, RU486 feels like a heavy period or an early miscarriage, and you may need some painkillers to feel more comfortable. It is also normal to feel headachey and sick and to have diarrhoea, though you should report these symptoms to a nurse.

The abortion is nearly always complete within six hours, and then you will be examined and discharged by the doctor. If you have not expelled the pregnancy by this time, you will probably be taken to theatre to have your womb cleaned out under a light general anaesthetic. Alternatively, you may be discharged to complete the abortion at home. This sounds worse than it is: remember that at this stage of pregnancy the foetus is usually invisible to the naked eye. But if you find this prospect upsetting, discuss your fears with a nurse or counsellor. You might want to arrange for someone to stay with you when you get home, just in case.

You will continue bleeding for a while, perhaps up to ten days. After a week you will need to go back to the hospital to check that your abortion is complete and that you are well.

RU486 allows you to have abortion at a very early stage of pregnancy; it can be a good option for women who prefer to avoid anaesthesia and invasive surgery. It is quite uncomfortable, however, and the repeated clinic visits can be very inconvenient. But perhaps more important is how you feel after being conscious during abortion. Many women prefer to wake up and find it all over, while others feel that staying conscious allows them to be more in control, and perhaps to come to terms with the experience more quickly.

VACUUM ASPIRATION/SUCTION

The vast majority of abortions up to 12 to 14 weeks' gestation are performed by vacuum aspiration. You will usually be under general anaesthetic – though some clinics will do it under local anaesthetic if you ask.

Once in hospital, you may have prostaglandin pessaries

inserted a few hours before the operation to help soften your cervix. You may also be given an injection which will help you to relax.

The operation itself takes just a few minutes. The surgeon will swab your vaginal area with disinfectant, and insert a speculum to hold your vagina open. S/he then holds your cervix (the neck of the womb) with a tenaculum and gently opens it up with slim rods known as 'dilators'. The extent of dilatation needed increases with the length of pregnancy, but is rarely wider than the width of a ball-point pen. The surgeon passes a thin plastic tube, attached to a suction machine, into your womb, and gently sucks the contents out. S/he will then carefully scrape out the womb with a small metal instrument called a curette, to make sure the abortion is complete.

Vacuum aspiration is usually performed under light general anaesthetic, lasting about ten to fifteen minutes. If you prefer, you can ask to have local anaesthetic instead: this carries less risk and you won't feel so sleepy and sick afterwards. Some surgeons don't like to perform abortion under local anaesthetic, however, so be aware that your request may be refused.

If you do have local anaesthetic, you will usually walk straight into the operating theatre, lie down and put your feet up into stir-rups. The surgeon will give you an injection into your cervix, and perform the operation as described. Many women appreciate being conscious through the abortion, and feel this helps them to come to terms with the experience quickly. Others find the noise of the suction machine upsetting and the dragging sensation in their womb uncomfortable: hopefully, the theatre staff will be experienced and sensitive to your feelings.

After the abortion you will feel period-type cramps and will be bleeding. You may also feel drowsy and quite sick. This will not last long.

DILATATION AND EVACUATION (D&E)

Abortion is usually performed by D & E between 12 and 16 weeks' gestation (up to 20 weeks in non-NHS clinics such as

BPAS). This will always be done under general anaesthetic. As with vacuum aspiration, your feet will be put in stirrups and a speculum inserted. The surgeon may have already softened your cervix with prostaglandin pessaries or infusion, and s/he will stretch open your cervix with dilator rods. The foetus is removed with forceps and the contents of the womb are gently scraped out. Some women worry that this might hurt the foetus: it is highly unlikely that the foetal nervous system is sufficiently developed for pain to be experienced at this stage – but in any case, it will be unconscious from the anaesthetic in your bloodstream.

D & E takes longer than vacuum aspiration: you will need a longer-acting anaesthetic and an overnight stay, and will experience cramps and wooziness afterwards. It is a very safe operation when performed by skilled and experienced surgeons, and a far better option for most women than medical induction (see below). Unfortunately, many surgeons are not prepared to offer this type of surgery – either because they find it distasteful or because they have insufficient practice to feel confident about performing it.

MEDICAL INDUCTION (MI)

After about 18 weeks of pregnancy, most abortions are carried out by medical induction (MI) though it may be offered to you as early as 13 weeks. This is in effect an early labour, lasting between six and twenty-four hours.

This labour can be brought on in a number of ways: the most common is by giving prostaglandin by vaginal pessaries, or by injection through your tummy into the womb. You will also be given an intravenous drip containing other drugs to speed up the process and stop you feeling sick. These drugs cause contractions similar to childbirth, and may be quite painful: you will be given painkillers, however, and sometimes sedatives as well. A nurse will stay with you while you expel the pregnancy, and you do not have to see the foetus. After delivery you may be taken to the operating theatre to have your womb gently scraped out under general anaesthetic. The entire process and recovery will usually mean that you stay in hospital for two or three days.

This can be a very difficult form of abortion, both physically and emotionally. You will need a lot of support throughout this experience – unfortunately, this is sometimes not forthcoming if you are in an NHS ward with women who are facing infertility or threatened miscarriage. In a specialist unit you are more likely to get sympathetic treatment, and may be allowed the company of a friend or partner.

Increasing public awareness of the importance of grieving has led to some women asking to see the foetus after an abortion. It may be that you feel this would help you come to terms with the abortion experience; if so, you should ask – preferably the counsellor or a sympathetic member of staff – *before* you go in for the abortion. They may say no, but increasingly staff are becoming sympathetic to such requests. It is important, however, that you think through what you are expecting to see and how you expect to gain from the experience.

SOME OTHER METHODS OF ABORTION

Some clinics offer a 'two-stage' D & E for abortions over 12 weeks. In this operation, which is always performed under general anaesthetic, a dilating substance based on seaweed is placed inside the cervix. This gently swells and opens the cervix over twenty-four hours, allowing the surgeon to later scrape out the contents of the womb with a curette.

Hysterotomy (removing the foetus through the uterine wall) and hysterectomy (removing the entire womb) used to be common forms of abortion; these days, they are usually only performed for a medical reason such as womb cancer.

STERILIZATION WITH ABORTION

Performing sterilization at the same time as abortion is not usually advisable, for two reasons. First, the physical risks are thought to be higher. Second, the emotionally charged experience of unplanned pregnancy is not the best time to make a considered, objective decision about a permanent operation. It may be advisable to combine the two where it is imperative that you do not become pregnant again and where you know you would have wanted to be sterilized anyway – for example, if it is physically dangerous for you to become pregnant. But you should *never* agree to sterilization as a condition of getting an abortion. Unfortunately, some women – and particularly black and working class women – have in the past been pressurized to do just that.

Disposal of the foetus

Many women are very concerned as to what happens to the foetus after abortion; some ask if they can take it home for burial. This is not usually allowed, as there are very strict rules covering the disposal of human tissue. The products of abortion are examined carefully to check the abortion is complete, and then they are cremated.

You may, however, be allowed to see the foetus before cremation, if that is what you wish. Hospitals have varying policies on this, and your request may be refused. Some, like BPAS, will comply with your wishes, but may discuss with you first what you are wanting to see and how you expect to feel about it (with the vast majority of abortions, the products of conception are simply not recognizable as a baby).

If you are sure that you want to do this, make your request clear to the counselling or nursing staff before you are put under anaesthetic, and preferably before the date of your operation.

AFTER THE OPERATION

When you wake up after the abortion you may feel weepy, sleepy, or elated. These are all after-effects of general anaesthetic, and will quickly pass. You will be encouraged to get up as soon as possible: most women find it a great comfort to sit in the dayroom talking until it is time to go home.

If you have been told you qualify for daycare treatment, you must have a friend or relative come to fetch you, and this is a good idea even if you are staying overnight. You should not drive for at least twenty-four hours after a general anaesthetic, so you may need to make arrangements about public transport or a taxi. You will want to take it easy for a while after the abortion, and it really is a good idea to marshal your friends and supporters around you for a few days.

If you have had an early abortion, you will be able to go back to work in a day or two, but later abortions will need longer recuperation (the clinic or hospital can give you a sick note). You should feel quite healthy but the anaesthetic can leave you a bit sleepy and nauseous for a few days. Office work should not usually be a problem, but heavy manual work or lifting should be avoided for at least a few days: if you need an excuse, tell your colleagues you've got back trouble.

Abortion is a very safe surgical procedure: however, any operation carries some risks and it is important that you take special care of yourself for a while. You may have been given antibiotic tablets at the hospital to prevent infection; if so, you should finish the course of tablets. Whether or not you have antibiotics, you can reduce the risk of infection by following these guidelines:

- **Avoid penetrative sex for six weeks. If this is not feasible, use a condom.**
- **If you have a choice, have showers rather than baths for the first few days.**
- **Don't go swimming until after your post-operative check.**
- **Use sanitary towels rather than tampons until after your post-operative check.**

You will usually carry on bleeding for some days after your abortion. This may stop after a few hours, or you may bleed intermittently until your next period or bleed fairly heavily for two or three weeks. You may also experience some period-type pains and pass clots on about the third day after your operation. **Almost any form of bleeding and cramps are normal providing they do not exceed what you would expect from a heavy period.** Normal painkillers such as paracetamol or aspirin may be taken, following instructions on the bottle or packet. If you are concerned for any reason, contact the clinic or hospital where you had the operation.

If you have had a medical abortion with RU486, you should not smoke or drink alcohol for a couple of days, and do not take pain-killers containing aspirin or ibuprofen until your follow-up check.

After an abortion many women declare that they will never have sex again – but nearly all of them do! Bear in mind that you are capable of becoming pregnant again *immediately* after the abortion, so have some contraception ready. The Pill may be started on the evening of the day of your operation or the following morning. Remember that missing pills, diarrhoea and vomiting, or antibiotics, may affect the absorption of the Pill – you will then need to take extra precautions.

You can have an IUD fitted at the time of the abortion, though some doctors think this may increase the risk of infection. If you have been using a cap or diaphragm, you will need to have the size checked; in any case, you should not use a female barrier method for at least 2 weeks after an abortion.

If you have had a very late abortion, the doctor may have prescribed a drug called Bromocryptine to dry up your milk supply. If s/he has not, your breasts may start to produce milk afterwards. It is best to wear a firm support bra day and night while your breasts are heavy and tender, along with breast pads or panty liners inserted inside the bra. Pain can be relieved by taking your normal pain reliever. Do **not** try to express milk as you will encourage further production. If you follow these instructions you will find the symptoms subside after a few days.

It is very important that you have a post-operative check after an abortion. This will usually be one week after an RU486 abortion, and up to six weeks after surgical termination. You will be given an appointment by the hospital or clinic that arranged your abortion, but if you prefer you can go to your own doctor or the Family Planning Clinic. This check is to make sure you have not picked up an infection and that you are definitely not pregnant. It is also an opportunity to talk to staff if you are feeling depressed or upset.

CHAPTER SIX

AFTER ABORTION

Abortion is a very safe operation. That does not mean that it is totally risk-free – no medical procedure ever is – but it is usually safer than driving a car, having your tonsils out, or having a baby.

Any operation can be worrying – and the prospect of general anaesthetic and invasive surgery can be frightening, particularly for young women who may never have been in hospital before. Sometimes knowledge helps, which is why we have set out to explain the main risks involved in abortion. If you are still concerned after reading this chapter, you may find it useful to talk through your fears with a trained counsellor or nurse.

PHYSICAL RISKS OF ABORTION

Your risk of suffering complications after abortion is strongly linked to the gestation of your pregnancy. Early abortion is very safe, while later terminations need a stronger anaesthetic and carry increased risk of tearing or overstretching the cervix.

Your level of risk will also be affected by your age, your general health including smoking habits, the type of operation you have and where you have it. Studies have shown that the NHS has a higher complication rate than the private sector: this is partly because the NHS is more likely to treat those women who have pre-existing medical problems, and partly because non-NHS surgeons tend to be more experienced and highly skilled.

About 5 per cent of women can expect to suffer minor complications after abortion (less for those under 12 weeks' gestation).

The most common risk is of **infection**, which can be easily cleared up with a course of antibiotics (you may be given these before you leave the hospital). If you have any pre-existing infections like chlamydia or a sexually transmitted disease, it is important to get them cleared up before the operation. These conditions are often symptomless; if for any reason you suspect you may be infected, tell the doctor.

Other minor complications are **retained products** of incomplete abortion and **cervical tears**: these can usually be dealt with before you leave the hospital, otherwise you will need to return to have them seen to under light general anaesthetic.

Major complications are *very* rare, but could include **haemorrhage, severe cervical tears, perforation of the uterus,** and **anaesthetic complications.** The death rate is about 1 in every 100,000 abortions. If this still sounds high to you – after all, we expect doctors to make us better, not worse – remember that the death rate for childbirth is about 8 in every 100,000.

Many women fear that abortion will damage their future ability to have children: this is something you should not worry about. Repeated and reputable research studies have shown that abortion does not cause infertility, miscarriage or problems in later pregnancies.

It is sometimes said that abortion is only as serious as having a tooth out: in terms of physical risk that is absolutely true, but this is not a helpful way of looking at this very stressful time in your life. The main concern at this point is usually not so much your physical health as your emotional well-being.

EMOTIONAL EFFECTS OF ABORTION

There has been a lot of public attention in recent years to a phenomenon called 'Post-Abortion Syndrome'. This is described as an emotional breakdown similar to that suffered by survivors of major disasters, when women who have had abortions are psychologically crippled by depression, guilt and inability to come to

106

terms with their experience. Many women attending clinics for abortion advice and help are now convinced that they will spend their lives in guilt and grieving for what they are choosing to do.

In truth, there is no medical evidence that supports the idea of 'Post-Abortion Syndrome'. As a specific psychological disorder, it simply does not exist. That is not to deny that many women feel very emotional and distressed after abortion – but these feelings are usually a short-lived and appropriate response to what is a very difficult time in their lives, not an indication of a psychological disorder caused by the termination.

It is statistically much safer in terms of psychological risk to have an abortion than to continue a pregnancy. About 10 per cent of women experience short-term minor depression after abortion; longer-term and more serious depression occurs in about 1–2 per cent. This more serious depression is statistically more likely if:

- You are very young.
- You have a history of depression.
- You have a late abortion.
- You are severely ambivalent.
- You are lonely and unsupported.
- You have low self-esteem.
- You have to terminate a wanted pregnancy – perhaps because of foetal abnormality or changed circumstances such as marital breakdown.

HOW WILL I FEEL AFTER THE ABORTION?

Women feel many things after abortions. You could feel relief, euphoria, depression, guilt, grief or anger. You may just feel numb for a while. Many people think that abortion will always be a negative choice and therefore you are bound to suffer afterwards. This denies the experience of those women who feel comfortable choosing termination and clear that they have the right to control their fertility. If your decision was straightforward you may be able to come to terms with it quite easily. It can be quite disconcerting when well-meaning people imagine you to be heartbroken or guilt-ridden.

It is also possible that you will experience a range of powerful and distressing emotions. Don't feel anxious that you should be reacting in a certain way. You should allow yourself to come to terms with your abortion in a way that seems right for you. You may worry that your feelings will become a burden that you will carry with you forever. This is unlikely to be true. You could find that once you have given yourself the freedom to express how you feel, you can begin to face the future without too many regrets.

Your feelings may come as a surprise to you. You might have been very sad before the termination but experience great relief once the operation is over. You may have found the choice easy to make, and yet be overwhelmed by guilt or sadness afterwards. If you are particularly distressed it could be for one or more of the following reasons:

- You did not feel in control of your decision.
- Someone else pressurized you into having the termination.
- You are coping with the end of a relationship or you are not happy in your relationship.
- The abortion has highlighted other problems in your life.
- You see the termination as a personal failure.
- Abortion is against your religious beliefs or your philosophy of life.
- You developed a strong relationship with the foetus.
- You longed to have a child but your circumstances made it impossible.
- You were not treated well by consultants and hospital staff or you were not supported by those who are close to you.

It will be useful to remind yourself of the reasons why you chose to have an abortion. At that time, feeling as you did, with the information you had, you made the decision you thought was right. If you do regret your decision, remember the pressure you were under at the time. Would it have really been feasible to continue the pregnancy? Allowing yourself to be positive about your choice and supporting your right to have made it can be a good starting point to explore more painful and complex feelings.

Because abortion is still relatively taboo, you may be dealing with difficult feelings in an atmosphere of secrecy or disapproval. You could feel that you don't deserve sympathy from yourself or other people and that you should just pull yourself together and get on with your life. Part of coping will be to accept that your feelings are valid and that you are entitled to support. You may want to begin by identifying what has made the abortion a difficult experience. The following exercise might help you to clarify this.

EXERCISE 1

Feelings afterwards

- **Write a list of statements beginning each one with 'I feel…'** Put down anything that comes into your head. They don't have to make sense and they can be contradictory, e.g., 'I feel really strong' and 'I feel frightened'.
- **Make a list of statements beginning with 'I should…'** – all the things that other people expect of you or you expect of yourself, e.g., 'I should be really sensible' or 'I should stop thinking about the abortion'.
- **Now make a third list of statements beginning 'I want…'** It doesn't matter what it is, or whether or not you can have it, e.g., 'I want to be left alone', 'I want my baby back', 'I want to feel good about myself'.
- **Read over your list of feelings.** If you can, write down some of the specific reasons why you feel these things. What aspects of the abortion make you feel particularly bad? Do other people's opinions of you come into the picture? Are your feelings connected to other things going on in your life?
- **Have a look at your list of 'I should's.** How much of a

strain is it going to be to live up to this? Cross out the ones you could live without. Look at the ones that are left. Are they realistic expectations? If they are very important, add them to the 'I want' list, e.g., 'I should be able to concentrate on work' becomes 'I want to be able to concentrate on work'.

- **Have another look at your 'I want...' list.** Are the things you want all things that you can't have? Or are they things you can ask for or get for yourself? If it is difficult to get them, what obstacles are standing in the way? Looking at your list of feelings may give you some clues as to why it's hard to get what you want. If you want to feel closer to your partner but you are feeling angry, this is not going to be easy.

Examining your feelings in this way will not make them go away but it will start to give you a clearer picture of where you are at the moment and what you might need from the future. It may help you understand what particular issues the abortion has brought up for you. These will be entirely personal and different from those of your best friend, your colleague or the woman down the road.

ALLOWING YOURSELF TO GRIEVE

Not every woman will need to grieve after an abortion but if you do, it is important that you allow yourself that right. When someone close to you dies or a relationship ends it is accepted that you will need time to mourn your loss before you can get on with your life. It is not so accepted that you may have similar feelings after an abortion – but many women do experience a great sense of bereavement.

This may be a confusing sort of grief to come to terms with. You have not lost a person but a potential person. How do you express that grief, even to yourself? What is it that you need to grieve for? Maybe it is the lost opportunity for motherhood, because of the pressure that made it so difficult to continue the pregnancy. Or perhaps you are mourning the end of your relationship with your partner. If you had a real sense of the foetus as the child you wanted to have, you may be mourning the end of that relationship also.

Acknowledging your grief can be a frightening prospect, especially if it implies that you regret your decision. If you have had to struggle to get the abortion or have had to deal with disapproval or lack of support, it can be hard to justify your feelings of sadness. **Grieving over your decision does not mean it was wrong.** The extent and the experience of grief after an abortion will vary greatly. Some women will experience it fleetingly at the time of the operation and then feel able to accept the termination and leave it behind as part of their life's experience. Others will carry a sense of loss with them for a long time. If you do feel a sense of loss, try not to feel threatened by it. No one can go through life without experiencing loss or sadness; the important thing is to be able to express it and ultimately feel comfortable with it. If you look back to other experiences of grief in your life, you will see that the emotional intensity of it has faded, even though it seemed at the time that it would go on for ever.

It is natural not to want to face up to painful emotion, but ironically, the more we deny our feelings the more pain they may cause us in the long run. Rather than struggling bravely through months of depression, lack of concentration and sleep, and unexplained problems in your relationship, it is more valuable to try to address the real source of your distress.

This is not to say that grieving is an easy or a straightforward process – it can often get bound up with other feelings such as anger or guilt. We tend to talk about grief in terms of death; it is partly this connection which makes it a frightening emotion. However, grief is present in life in lots of different ways: finishing a relationship, losing a job, growing older or growing apart from a close friend or a parent. Grieving about your abortion doesn't happen in isolation. Your sense of loss will be in context with regrets you have about your past, hopes for the future and feelings about yourself.

EXERCISE 2
How you grieve

Look back to another experience of grief in your past. It can be big or small but something that made you feel very sad for a while.

- **How did you behave then?** Do you remember how you felt? Is the experience of grieving for the abortion similar or different?
- **What other emotions are involved with your grief?** Do you feel angry, sad, bitter? Is the sense of loss specifically centred on the abortion or is it connected with other times, other losses?
- **How long did it take you to come to terms with the loss in your first experience?** Do you feel good about how you came to terms with it, or does it make you feel anxious just to think about it? What did you learn from it?
- **What helped you get through it?** Could that be helpful now? Looking back, did you struggle on alone when you could have asked for support? With hindsight, what would have been the best way of looking after yourself? Are you able to use that information to look after yourself now?

It will be easier for you if the people around you understand how you feel. Grief can be frightening and sometimes even embarrassing. You may feel that you cannot expect endless support from the people around you and that you are behaving unreasonably if you cannot just have one good cry and get over it. You may need to make it clear to your partner or friends that you will need their support for some time.

As we said earlier, the majority of women do not experience long-term trauma over abortion. Facing up to your loss honestly and without judging yourself can often help you find the strength to accept it. Perhaps this will be a private process or perhaps it is something you can share with those closest to you.

Some women choose to join a support group. Talking with other women who have had abortions can stop you from feeling isolated or that no one understands what you've been through. Listening to other women's experiences may also give you insight in how to deal with your own. You could decide to see a counsellor or a therapist after the termination. One or two sessions might be enough or you could choose to see someone on a regular basis for a while.

If you are unable to come to terms with the abortion over a long period of time, you will need to decide whether you can live comfortably with such a great sense of loss. It is likely that the abortion has touched on a deep nerve and you may want to explore what this is and to question why it is so hard for you to live with the decision that you have made.

Your loss will also be affected by your relationship to the foetus. This can depend on the length of your pregnancy. Some women are very distressed by the changes in their body or seeing the foetus on a scan. You may have an image in your mind of an actual baby whose potential life you have terminated. You could find yourself having fantasies about what your child would have been like, wondering if it would have been a boy or a girl and feeling cheated because the abortion has taken away this experience from you. It may be particularly painful for you to be around babies and small children, or you might be drawn to them to stay in touch with your loss.

If the foetus, or the baby you have created in your mind, is very real to you, then part of your grieving process may be the need to say goodbye. There are no rituals associated with abortion; there is nowhere to lay flowers and no established ceremony where you can share your sadness with others. This means that some women are left with a sense of emptiness once the operation is over. It is for you to decide whether ritual is important and, if it is, to create your own. Decide what you would like to do. It could be very simple, like lighting a candle. It could involve going alone or with friends or partner to a favourite place and devising your own cere-mony. It is about finding your own way of saying goodbye.

Saying goodbye is also about letting go. You may hold on to your grief for a number of reasons. You could have a need to punish yourself, or be frightened of the future. You might be avoiding looking at other problems in your life. Feelings do change in time and coping with a profound loss is not always a negative experience. It can strengthen your relationships and help you understand yourself more clearly. You cannot alter the past but you do have control over your future. Allowing yourself to grieve in a way which is not destructive, can help you to regain control over your life.

GUILT AND SELF-ESTEEM

There seems to be an expectation that most women will feel guilty about having a termination. This is not necessarily true – many women are clear that there is no need to blame themselves. However, if you are aware of these expectations, you may feel guilty for not feeling guilty, as if there is something callous and coldhearted in refusing to punish yourself for your decision.

If you don't feel guilty, you are not unnatural or hard and you are likely to have a much easier time coming to terms with the abortion. If you do feel guilty, it may be useful to look at where the guilt stems from and the effect it may have on you in the future. Which of the following are the likely sources of your guilt?

- **Fear of other people's disapproval. Imagining what your mother or the neighbours or the rabbi would say.**
- **Feeling that you have been stupid or that you have let yourself down.**

114

- Feeling that you have done something that is morally wrong.
- Seeing the abortion as just one more failure in a whole line of personal failures.
- Feeling selfish – or putting your own needs first.

Guilt can lead to the belief that you are bad, stupid, or worthless. If you feel very guilty, you may feel you deserve punishment rather than support. Guilt is a very negative emotion and can be hell to live with. It is also something most of us are familiar with. Who or what has made you feel guilty in the past? Is it your religion? Your community's or parents' expectations? Is it the fear that you don't quite measure up, that you are never good enough? Is it the uphill struggle to behave like Superwoman?

Having an abortion can mean fighting for what you want, sometimes against religious or cultural or other people's expectations. It may mean disregarding people's disapproval, or your parents' wish for grandchildren. An abortion can highlight your feelings about being a woman, your sexuality, your relationship or lack of one, and your attitude to motherhood and children. It is possible, when faced with all this, that your complex feelings can become intensely self-punishing.

If you think you are deserving of punishment, then you may begin to create punishing situations for yourself. Some women punish themselves by staying in failing or abusive relationships, getting pregnant again in equally difficult circumstances, or by regarding themselves as unworthy of support or help.

In Chapter Two, 'Making Your Decision', we looked at how it is important to banish the self-punishing voice in order to make the right decision. Sometimes it is harder to get rid of that voice after the termination because now you have made your decision and have to live with it. If you feel stuck with your guilt the following exercise may be helpful.

EXERCISE 3
Dealing with guilt

- **Write down a list of statements beginning 'I feel guilty because...'** Put down as many as you can. Are you feeling guilty because you failed to live up to your own expectations or someone else's? Or because you don't think much of yourself and therefore any decision is bound to be wrong?

- **Imagine a child sitting in a room.** Perhaps the child is you when you were younger, or perhaps it is just a symbol of the vulnerable side of you. Look at the list of things you feel guilty about and, in your imagination, turn them into accusations and shout them at the child, e.g., 'I feel guilty because I made a stupid mistake' becomes 'How could you make such a stupid mistake!' Say them over and over if you want to and be as vitriolic as you like.

- **What happens to the child in the image?** Does she cry under the attack? Or sulk? Or cower? Or a combination of these? Is she able to defend herself?

- **It is probably fairly clear that if you treated a real child in this way she would not grow up to be confident, happy, or successful in what she chose to do.** Imagine what it feels like to be on the other end of this attack. This is what you may be living with right now. Note the child's reaction. Perhaps there is a similarity with how you have been feeling. If the child just stares blankly out of the window, perhaps you have reacted in the same way by being depressed and listless. If the child is shaking with fear, maybe this echoes the 'irrational' panic attacks you have been having, or your lack of conviction about coping with your life.

- **What happens to the child when you stop shouting at her?** How would it feel to ask the child what she needs at the moment?

- **It may feel stupid to ask her what she needs.** It may be that you do not want to know, or you are too angry with her to care. But you won't know until you ask.

- **If you do ask or you can guess what the child's needs are, are you going to be able to provide what she wants?** Probably not all at once. Perhaps you have to make a compromise with her. Can you at least stop punishing her? How can you start to look after her?

Of course, it won't be an easy task to change old habits of self-criticism. Guilt is usually not particularly rational. We all know that, if we wake up in the morning feeling weepy and depressed, we can't just tell ourselves to be happy and snap out of it. But if you start by seeing guilt as a choice rather than an inevitability, then at least this opens up the possibility that you can make different choices.

We are usually conditioned to be hard on ourselves. Self-punishment can even look like mature behaviour from the outside. Approving of yourself can seem soppy or fairly ridiculous. It isn't. It's essential. No one else's support will be as important as your own. If you want to, you can choose to be guilty about your abortion forever. Perhaps the important question is, who would benefit if you did? Certainly not you.

BUILDING SELF-ESTEEM

It is important that you do not let the abortion undermine your self-esteem. Low self-esteem can be a vicious circle. When we feel bad about ourselves, we may put up with lousy relationships and sex which we don't enjoy, and allow ourselves to be dumped on at work or by our children or parents or spouses. Then when this happens, it is further proof of what we already knew: that we are weak, pathetic creatures who only deserve what we get.

In this scenario, unplanned pregnancy can seem like just one more personal failure. You may blame yourself for not using birth control, for having sex in the first place, or for not being able to cope with having a child. Rather than recognizing that your expectations of yourself may be too high or allowing yourself to make the occasional mistake, you could use the circumstances of your pregnancy as evidence that you are not good enough. It is then possible you will seek similar situations (however unconsciously) just to prove your point to yourself over again.

EXERCISE 4
Building your self-esteem

What was your image of yourself like before you got pregnant?
Has having an abortion changed that image?

- **Write down as many words as you can that describe you.** Anything that comes into your head.
- **Make two lists, one of six positive things about yourself and another six negative things.** Notice what happens when you do this? Is it easier to think of the negative? How complimentary are you being with the positive? Are they things you like about yourself or are they what other people like about you?
- **Reread what you have written.** What does it tell you about how you see yourself? Are you someone you would like to know?
- **Make a third list, this time of things you would like to be.** Try not to turn it into things you *should* be.
- **Which list best sums up how you feel about yourself right now?** Which list sums up the woman who got pregnant and had an abortion?
- **Look at the third list – things you would like to be – and imagine what the woman would look like.** How would she be coping at the moment? What would she want from her life and her relationships? What advice would she give to someone in your situation?

- **Reread the list of positive characteristics.** Remember that these are just as much part of you as the negative ones. Imagine that you already have the qualities that you would like to have. How does that make you feel? Maybe you are already some of those things, perhaps not all the time, but sometimes. If this is not true then how does it feel to want to be very different than you are now?
- **How difficult is it to feel good about yourself?** What do you need to do to make it easier?

LOOKING AFTER YOURSELF

Looking after yourself can mean: exploring your feelings in a way that is safe for you; not punishing yourself or dismissing your feelings as irrelevant or stupid; being able to ask for the support that you need; accepting that an abortion can be a painful loss for you or a straightforward and positive decision or anything in between; making your physical and emotional well-being a priority.

- **Make a list of things that you like to do.** Things that make you feel good about yourself. Add to the list things you may need from other people.
- **Look at your list and decide which are the easiest to put into practice.** They could be as simple as having a morning to yourself, watching your favourite TV programme or soaking in a bubble bath. Make sure that you find some time to do them.
- **What about what you need from other people?** Is it likely you will be able to get the time and attention you need? Even if you can't get everything you want, are you prepared to ask for some of it?
- **What about the things you would like to but feel you can't have at the moment?** Is it possible to compromise? Maybe you would like to go to bed for a week and can't – but you could give yourself a day or a morning. Perhaps you would like a long holiday and can't afford it or can't take the time off – but you

could go away for the weekend or at least try and plan a holiday in the near future.

SUPPORT

How supportive are the people around you? Do you prefer to keep your feelings to yourself or will it help you to talk to others about the termination? Do your nearest and dearest feel you should forget about it all and get on with your life or do they accept that you may need some time?

Sometimes we feel too guilty to burden our friends with our worries and so keep them all to ourselves; at other times friends tell us in no uncertain terms that there is only so much they can take. Finding the right balance isn't always easy but if you trust the people around you then there should be room for give and take.

EFFECT ON RELATIONSHIPS

If your partner supported you in making your own decision or if the decision was shared, then you have a good basis for resolving difficulties later. You may even find that the abortion will bring you closer together, especially if you are both able to talk openly about your feelings. If there is already conflict in the relationship or your views on the pregnancy were opposed then it could be harder to resolve your differences.

If you feel angry and betrayed by your partner, then it is unlikely that these feelings will simply go away. Leaving a relationship, however, is not always an easy decision. You may have been together a long time, be financially dependent on him, or you might be frightened of facing the future alone. You may also be committed to your partner and want to make the relationship work. Most adult relationships are not simply either good or bad. They can be complex and it can take effort and time to sort out the problems between you.

Even if your partner has been supportive, this does not guarantee you will have an easy time. You could feel that he expects you to feel the same as you did before the abortion. It is possible that you will be angry, distant or terribly clingy and insecure. You might be apologetic about this or believe that he simply has no idea what you have been through. He could feel guilty or bewildered by your response to the abortion. He may feel left out or imagine that his feelings don't count. He might think you are being irrational or too demanding and resent you you getting support from other people. He may feel like a total heel.

A real man, so we are led to believe, does not cry, is always strong and in control. Because of this, lots of women are the emotional caretakers in their relationships. They are the ones who bolster self-esteem, who wipe away tears and who can talk about feelings. It can be a big challenge to your partner if you are vulnerable and perhaps in need of sensitive support. If you are used to doing all the caring then you could find it difficult to ask for what you need.

It may be useful to think about what you want from the relationship and to clarify some of your feelings when you are alone or with a close friend or someone you trust. If you firmly believe that your partner is an insensitive pig who will never understand you then perhaps you need to ask yourself why you are staying in this relationship. There may be important reasons why you are, in which case you will need to look elsewhere for your emotional support.

If you want your partner's support and understanding then you should be able to ask for, and have some expectation of getting, what you want. You will both have to find ways of expressing how you feel honestly, without it being seen as a threat.

COMMUNICATION

It is possible that once you've had the operation your partner will believe that it is all over. For you it may not be. Even if the abortion has not been particularly traumatic, you may want to talk about it, to get it into perspective. You might also feel there is pressure on you to get back to normal as quickly as possible. What you will need from your partner is a real understanding of how you might be feeling. That does not mean he has to feel the same, but he should be able to acknowledge if you are upset or confused or angry. The less your partner really accepts this, the more you will be tempted to take your feelings out on him instead of trying to share them.

Try to be clear about what you want. If he keeps trying to change the subject when you want to talk, then say so, rather than harbour a lot of resentment. Try to explain how you feel in a way that is not apologetic but that does give your partner some insight.

If every conversation ends in a row or simply fizzles out, perhaps you both need some time apart to work out what you want and what is going wrong between you. If you can discuss problems constructively, set aside some time to do this and remember some of the things you enjoy doing together as a couple. The more comfortable you are together, the easier it will be to discuss painful issues.

If it's only you who is open, while he sits there saying nothing, you could feel vulnerable or imagine that you are the one with all the problems. It will be easier if you are both able to talk about your response to the termination. Listen to each other without thinking that you have to take responsibility for each other's feelings. If you are angry, be as specific as you can about what made you angry and why.

Your relationship will probably have changed after the abortion in some way. You have considered becoming parents and decided that now is not the right time. Because of this, you will have talked or at least thought about your future together. There may be all sorts of issues flying around. Are we going to stay together? Are we going to have children in the future? Do we want the same things from this relationship? These are all big questions and you probably will not resolve them straight away. It might not be a brilliant idea to sit down and try to sort out the rest of your lives together if you're feeling angry or upset after the abortion. On the other hand, carrying on pretending nothing has happened is stressful and if it goes on long enough, you could end up behaving like two strangers.

If you and your partner are having problems it might be useful to consider the following points:

- **Be as clear as you can about what your expectations are.** Do not waste huge amounts of emotional energy trying to get what is not on offer.
- **Be as honest as you dare.** That way you both know where you stand.
- **If you are punishing your partner for the abortion,** think about what has made you so angry with him and what effect this may have on the relationship.
- **Try not to dismiss what your partner is saying** and do not let him dismiss what you are saying. Understanding another's point of view does not mean that yours is wrong.
- **Ask for what you want,** whether it's lots of affection, time on your own or time to talk about specific issues.
- **Don't apologize for how you feel.**
- **Remember that being hurt or angry with each other does not mean the relationship is doomed.** This could be a time when either or both of you need reassurance that you still care and are committed to working things out.
- **You may both need other support.** Sometimes men find it hard to talk about personal issues to their friends. If you usually provide all your partner's emotional support, he may want to think about seeing a counsellor.
- **If you're stuck in a rut, endlessly rowing or unable to resolve things constructively, think about couple counselling.** Relate offers free relationship counselling. They will see couples together and individually. Other counselling agencies may also offer couple counselling (see Help and Information, p. 174).

SEX AND SEXUALITY

It is not uncommon for women to say they never want sex again after an abortion. Of course, it is unlikely you will opt for a lifetime of celibacy, but the abortion may affect the way you feel about yourself, your body and your sex life. This can happen for one or more of the following reasons:

- If you feel guilty about the abortion, you may start to feel guilty about your sex life.
- You could be anxious to avoid another unplanned pregnancy and find that this fear undermines your enjoyment of sex.
- If you experienced the abortion as an invasion of your body and of your privacy, sex might seem like a similar invasion. This could depend on how you are treated by the clinic or hospital. If you were made to feel embarrassed or cheap, or had an internal examination done by insensitive doctors, it could be difficult for you to feel good about your body.
- You might not feel sexual at the moment. You may want to take time to come to terms with the termination physically and emotionally. You may want to avoid sexual contact as a way of protecting yourself and regaining a sense of control.
- The abortion might have affected the way you feel about your partner (or potential partners).

Whatever you feel, take your time. On a practical level, you should avoid intercourse for six weeks after the abortion, because of the risk of infection. Emotionally, it may take you longer to feel like having sex. You might worry that you will never enjoy sex again, that you will be described as frigid or that your partner will become angry and frustrated. It is important to talk through your feelings with your partner and to explain that you are not withholding sex as a punishment. Sex is supposed to be about pleasure and there is no point in agreeing to have sex unless you are going to enjoy it.

You do not have to have sex to be close to your partner. Try and ask for what you need – it could be lots of affection and cuddles or spending time together doing things you enjoy. If you feel under pressure to have sex you are likely to panic even more.

If you are feeling guilty about the abortion, or see it as a personal failure this could lead to feeling uncomfortable about your sexuality. We get powerful messages about how we should behave sexually, and many of them are negative. Think back to when you were younger. What was your parents' attitude to sex? How did they talk about pregnancy and abortion, if at all? What about your friends? What rumours and stories were there about girls who got pregnant, who had sex before they were married or when they were 'too young' or with too many, or the wrong sort of people? The messages you received when you were younger will still be part of you. Regaining your confidence about your sexuality will be part of the process of coming to terms with the abortion.

Another reason you may not feel good about sex is your fear of another unwanted pregnancy. If you were not using birth control before, you might worry that no contraceptive is 100 per cent reliable. If you were using birth control, you could feel if it went wrong once, what is to stop it going wrong again?

If the abortion was a difficult experience, you will want to go to great lengths to avoid it happening again. Realistically, that means making careful choices about birth control (see Chapter Nine, 'Contraception') but emotionally it could mean giving yourself time to allay the anxiety. Sex is unlikely to be relaxed and fun, if all your thoughts are centred on the abortion or if you are nervously counting the days to your next period. You could choose to avoid intercourse for a while and to explore different (and safer) ways of giving each other sexual pleasure.

Feeling good about your sexuality is just as important if you are single or do not have a regular sexual partner. You may find that you are reluctant to get involved with anyone until you have worked through your feelings about the abortion. You should regard this as a positive choice rather than an admission of failure. Neither should you feel guilty about starting a new relationship, if this is what you want.

You may find that you want to have sex, perhaps with different partners, in order to feel desired and wanted or to boost your self-esteem. Try and be clear with yourself what you are looking for. If it is reassurance and affection then you might not find this in fleeting sexual encounters. One-night stands and brief affairs do not have to be damaging, but they can be, if you are feeling vulnerable or you are trying to prove that you are not worth very much. You deserve to have sexual relationships that make you feel good about yourself.

Remember . . .

- Give yourself as much time as you need to feel you are in control. You will not feel good about having sex when you do not want to have it.
- Allow yourself to feel OK about *not* being sexual. Don't let it panic you.
- Allow yourself to feel OK about being sexual. Having an abortion does not take away your right to enjoy sex. See what negative guilt feelings are getting in your way.
- Negotiate with your partner. Do not allow your partner to exert pressure on you. Find other ways of being close and physical with each other.
- Pay special attention to your body. Look after it, it has had a rough time. What makes it feel good? It could be massage, sleep, swimming, walking, a hot bath. Try to pamper yourself as much as you can.

POST-ABORTION COUNSELLING

Some women come to terms with their abortions alone or with the support of friends and partners. Others find it useful to seek counselling afterwards. If you continue to be distressed or guilty after an abortion then it could be helpful to see a counsellor. It is important that you do not see getting help as an admission of failure. It can be hard to face up to difficult and complex emotions alone and even the most supportive people in your life cannot be totally objective.

Seeing a counsellor does not provide a magic answer. What it does offer is a place where you can focus on your feelings and the issues that the abortion has brought up. It may require you to be honest with yourself in order to identify and tackle the real problems. A counsellor can help you do this in a way that is constructive and where you remain in control.

There is no right time to get post-abortion counselling. One or two sessions soon after the termination might be all that you need. You might feel fine for months, then start to realize that there are unresolved issues that you want to sort out. Sometimes counselling will be very centred on the abortion, but at other times the abortion will have only been the trigger for other things: maybe your relationships or your feelings about yourself. If this is the case, you might want to explore these wider issues over a longer period with a counsellor or therapist.

It is not an easy process talking to a complete stranger about your innermost thoughts and feelings. Usually it takes some time to build up trust. It is also important to find the right person. Counselling and therapy techniques vary greatly and every individual will have their own approach. What may work well for someone else might be unhelpful for you. Most long-term counsellors or therapists will suggest an initial 'interview'. This is a time for both of you to decide if you can work together.

Like abortion, counselling and therapy are not freely available on the National Health Service. However, the pregnancy advisory charities all offer post-abortion counselling and there are many voluntary agencies up and down the country who offer free or low-cost counselling. If you're under 26, you can go to the Brook Advisory Centre who can tell you what is on offer in your area, otherwise the British Association for Counselling has comprehensive lists of both free and private counselling organizations (see Help and Information, p. 174).

You can contact these agencies yourself. If you want NHS counselling you usually need to be referred by a GP. Although some therapists and counsellors are very expensive, many have fees on a sliding scale and you can negotiate with them how much you can afford to pay.

If you think counselling is a waste of time, too expensive, self-indulgent or only for unstable people, think again. It is actually much more sensible and practical to seek help in order to come to terms with painful emotions rather than spend months and even years feeling depressed or angry with yourself.

CHAPTER SEVEN

CHOOSING MOTHERHOOD

Choosing to continue your pregnancy and have a child will probably turn out to be the most important decision you ever make. You may well face other difficult choices – over jobs, homes, relationships – but they are not likely to affect as many other people, or be as irreversible, as this one.

Mixed in with your worries and concerns, you will probably also feel excited and positive about your pregnancy. Welcoming a new baby can be very draining, however, and you will enjoy those first few months more if you can sort out some of the practicalities in advance: this chapter will help you to explore your doubts and fears, and then tackle them.

DOUBTS AND FEARS

In any pregnancy, it is normal to experience mood swings that will leave you feeling joyful, anxious, and depressed by turn. This is partly due to the hormonal changes taking place in your body. Romantic fiction and advertising paint a fantasy picture of pregnancy that is often far removed from the messy reality of morning sickness and varicose veins: nevertheless, this fantasy may feel especially distant if your pregnancy was unplanned.

You could, for example, feel upset that you have 'missed out' on the joys of planned pregnancy. This is particularly likely if you have no partner, or if you are not practically prepared for a baby, or if your family and friends are not celebrating with you. Maybe, particularly if you are young and/or single, you are surrounded by people who are telling you that you are throwing your life away, and that you will never be able to provide your child with a proper home.

These attitudes may compound your own fears for the future. Bringing up children is not easy, and you do have to be prepared to make some sacrifices and to put in a lot of hard work. But it is also easy to let these natural concerns grow out of all proportion, particularly in the months before your baby actually arrives, when your own nervous anticipation and other people's real or imagined criticism of your unplanned pregnancy can conspire to haunt you with two of the most frequent asked and least answerable questions known to mothers: one is 'Have I made the right decision?', the other, 'Will I be a good enough mother?' We will now look at each of these questions in turn.

HAVE I MADE THE RIGHT DECISION?

It may be impossible to really know if motherhood is right for you until you've tried out the experience for yourself. You could find it easier to make an informed choice if you've got some practical information about what help will be available to you, and if you have spent time around other mothers and small children. But even then you can't be certain, because your child, and your experience of motherhood, will be different from anyone else's. You probably know among your own family and friends one woman who found childbearing the most profound and creative project of her life, another who loves her children but regrets the loss of income and personal freedom, and a third who would have been better off if she'd stayed childless. Choosing motherhood is like *Blind Date* with a vengeance, as you are taking on a lifelong relationship with someone you've never even met!

There may well be times when you regret your decision – particularly as you have to adjust to not being on your own any more during the first few months, or during the 'terrible twos' and teenage tantrums – but this will not necessarily mean that the choice you made was wrong. Women who choose **not** to continue unplanned pregnancies also sometimes feel regret, and wonder if they have missed out on the satisfactions of parenthood. Whichever way you have chosen, you will find problems and rewards, so try not to look back with regrets.

The choice between motherhood and abortion can be so difficult for some women that they drift through an unplanned pregnancy without ever having made a proper decision. Instead, they chew over their dilemma endlessly until it is too late for abortion; they have, in effect, chosen motherhood by default. It is far better if you can make a positive choice to turn an unplanned pregnancy into a wanted child – and start planning life accordingly – than to let yourself feel like a victim of circumstance.

Finally, try and keep a sense of perspective about the choice you have made. Whichever way you have chosen, you will probably have an all right, up-and-down sort of life like everyone else: research on people over fifty has shown no difference in happiness or satisfaction between mothers and childless women. If you are worried that having been unplanned will disadvantage your baby, remember that nearly half of all loved and wanted children started out as unplanned pregnancies. Our mothers shared the doubts and fears that you are feeling now – and we all survived!

THE MYTH OF THE MOTHER

Motherhood is such an awesome project that many of us feel insecure and unsure about whether are are up to the job. There are a lot of myths about the role, many of them very damaging and hurtful to those families who do not fit 'the norm'. For example, immigrant women often feel their own cultural traditions of childbearing are misunderstood and disapproved of by Western professionals, while lesbian households are branded as 'pretend family relationships' in law.

Even if you do not face the disapproval of wider society, you may feel undermined and belittled by your own family and friends who doubt your ability to parent. It can seem like everyone else is an expert on how to raise your child – but that all its faults and misdemeanours will be blamed on you.

What does good mothering mean to you? Think back to what was important in your own childhood, and to what was missing. If those important factors included love, stability, and adults who would listen to you and to each other, then you can feel reassured that you have the same kind of ideas as most childcare experts.

YOUR ASSETS

Think of the things you can offer your child. These don't have to be grand promises like 'everlasting love' or 'a car on his/her seventeenth birthday'. It could be that:

- People have always said you were good with children.
- You have a circle of friends who will make great 'aunties' and 'uncles'.
- You can offer grandparents who will love your baby to bits.
- You tell wonderful bedtime stories.

Don't underestimate your talents and abilities: you might not rate them much, but your child will.

YOUR NEEDS

It is also helpful to think through your own practical needs, both before and after the birth.

- Who do you want with you throughout labour?
- Do you have someone who will help take care of the shopping and cooking during the first few days or weeks?
- Do you have friends who will agree to babysit one night a week, so that you can go out and have some social life?
- Who can you talk to about your hopes and fears?

Don't neglect these needs: looking after yourself will help you to look after and enjoy your baby.

Remember, it is quite natural to have these fears about parenting – and usually more helpful to think them through than to ignore them. For some specific worries, identifying them early in pregnancy allows you time to find ways of dealing with them. For example, you can help prepare your children for the new baby, or look round for a bigger flat, or negotiate with your boss about returning to work.

Other concerns may be more 'cosmic': you may find yourself fretting over the possibility of nuclear war, or worried that you will become bored, boring and lonely. You may fear that there will be 'something wrong' with your baby, or that your relationship will never be the same, or that you won't cope with the pain of childbirth. There may not be a lot you can do about these worries, but just bringing them into the open, and talking them over, may help you feel better.

PLANNING AHEAD

Identifying your worries can be used as positive impetus to start planning for the future. Try not to worry too much: if you are prepared to make some sacrifices in exchange for the pleasures of parenthood, and if you are realistic about the changes it will make to your life, you should find motherhood rewarding. It is important that you use the months of pregnancy to do some forward-planning, though, so that you and your baby can have the best possible start together.

Whether you already have children, or are embarking on a whole new venture, you will need to think through what help you will need in the months and years ahead. It is a good idea for you (and your partner, if you have one) to survey your lifestyle and assess areas for improvement. Below we have set out some questions you could be asking yourself: they may not all be appropriate to you, but they will get you started. Once you have identified your needs you are forewarned – and can perhaps get some practical help in solving any difficulties.

SINGLE PARENTING

If you are on your own:

- **Do you have the financial and practical resources necessary to raise a child?**
- **Will your family and friends offer just occasional babysitting, or do any of them see their part in your child's life as significant?**
- **Who can you call at three in the morning if your baby won't stop crying and you just can't cope?**
- **How will the baby affect your social life, future relationships, and career plans?**

Over one-quarter of all babies are born to unmarried women, and one in three marriages ends in divorce, so single parenting is very common in this country (and in many others). Yet single parents are favourite scapegoats of politicians and journalists who claim that single parenting leads to juvenile delinquency and urban crime. If you are single and pregnant, this kind of scare story can make you feel very apprehensive about what the future will hold for you and your child.

It is true that a high number of single parents live in poverty and isolation, and that it is far more difficult to provide a comfortable standard of living when you have no one to help you provide for your child. It doesn't matter if you can't afford the latest toys and trainers: the most important factor in your child's development will be its relationship with you; a happy and loving home life will usually outweigh any material disadvantage. Parenting is very hard work, however, and it may be more difficult for one parent than for two to give a child all the care and attention it will need. There is the risk of loneliness – both for you and for your child – and there is the risk that neither of you gets to mix with a sufficient variety of other adults. However wonderful your relationship with your child, it cannot be a substitute for adult friendships. Many of the problems faced by singe parents are linked with being isolated and unsupported, so it is valuable to work out in advance how you can get adult support. This may be from the child's biological father living elsewhere, or another partner, or family and friends. 'Help' is not the same as shared responsibility, but it can make all the difference between enjoying parenting and just coping.

If this sounds very gloomy, remember that most children of single-parent families do perfectly well, and many children of two-parent families do not. All families have problems, and you need psychic powers to work out if you are running a greater risk to start out single than to start out as a couple and risk divorce and family breakdown.

Practical help
If you are a single parent you can claim One Parent Benefit, in addition to other benefits (see p. 140). You can also claim Single Parents Tax Allowance and Additional Personal Allowance.

If you are a single parent you can also claim **child support** from the child's father. If you are claiming income support, family credit or disability living allowance, this is compulsory unless you can show a good reason for not having anything to do with your child's father (for example if you have reason to be scared of his violence). The Child Support Agency will assess and set the level of maintenance due to be paid to you; this will be counted against any benefits you may be claiming.

WHAT ABOUT THE FATHER?

'Shotgun weddings' – getting married only because you are pregnant – are very unfashionable these days. There is far less social stigma attached to unmarried motherhood, and increasing conviction that marriage should not be hurried into. If you are considering this step, pause to think through whether you would want to marry this man at this time if you were not pregnant. If you would, congratulations. If not, think again.

We hear that families 'need' fathers, but this is a relatively new idea, and in many parts of the world, including this country, children manage perfectly well without their fathers. But if you are considering bringing up your child totally on your own, you should consider how you will deal with future questions. Many children *do* want to know their biological father, and you should plan for this eventuality. You may, of course, wish to continue being involved with the father in some kind of relationship or friendship – marriage is not the only choice. But if you don't want to continue seeing the father, you could consider discussing with him his future involvement with the child.

If he is interested, then it is advisable to let him and the child know each other. This can be difficult: you might be very angry with him; you may feel jealous and threatened by his relationship with your child; you may want to punish him or use access as a bargaining tool for maintenance; or you may worry about him being irresponsible, letting your child down in some way.

- How will you divide childcare?
- Should you get married, or do you want a different kind of relationship?
- Do you have similar ideas on childrearing?
- Could you benefit from relationship counselling?

Unplanned pregnancy can be difficult: if you are in conflict with your partner, it may be traumatic. We have already explored some of these problems in Chapter Three, 'Conflict with Yourself and with Others', but now is the time to try and get these difficulties ironed out. Even if you cannot see eye-to-eye, you might find counselling or mediation services will help you come to some practical consensus on how to go forward as parents.

Many couples look forward to their baby with the firm conviction that they will not let parenthood change their lives – and are then shocked and disappointed at how much their style is cramped in the months following birth. It is important to be realistic, and to expect that you will both have to make some compromises in your personal freedom. You will also have to share each other with a very demanding third partner, and at times either one of you may feel jealous and excluded.

Try to negotiate in advance how you plan to share housework and childcare: it is all to easy to slip into a 'mothering' role which excludes your partner and exhausts you, because you do not trust him to care properly for the baby, or to clean the house up to your standards. Shared childcare means shared responsibility – it won't work if you can't 'let go' a bit. It may be, of course, that he is very reluctant to share in childcare – especially in the messy bits – because he sees it as 'women's work': if that is the case, you need to have this one out before the birth, to allow time for negotiation.

Much of this will depend on how you divide working arrangements. If you stay at home after the birth, it may be very difficult to persuade him to share housework and childcare with you. Even if you are working as well, the best laid plans can falter in the face of his larger pay packet or both your feelings that somehow his work and his time is more important than yours. These are horribly common feelings for all of us – watch out for them!

MOTHERS WITH DISABILITIES

- **Are you physically able to care for your child, or will you need extra help?**
- **Is that extra help forthcoming?**
- **Are there risks to your own health in continuing this pregnancy?**
- **Will your doctor and midwife treat you with respect and sensitivity? If not, what can you do about it?**
- **How can you help your child to face up to prejudice?**
- **What will your child lose by having a disabled mother?**
- **What will your child gain by having a disabled mother?**

Our society has difficulty coping with disability because there is a lot of fear and misunderstanding of disabled people. It is assumed that physical handicap involves mental impairment or psychological inadequacy, and that disabled people should be kept out of sight, or at least conform to a passive, sweet-natured 'victim' role.

Many people – doctors included – feel uncomfortable with the idea of disabled people being sexually active at all, and that it is irresponsible of women with disabilities to become pregnant or consider parenting. This is partly because of fear that the disability will be inherited, but mainly because it is assumed that these women cannot be 'fit mothers'. You may be made to feel guilty for supposedly inflicting your disability on your children, and under pressure to be a 'supermum' – always smiling, uncomplaining and brave.

Women with disabilities often face intense pressure to terminate pregnancies. It can be very difficult to continue a pregnancy – particularly if it was unplanned or if you are on your own – when doctors and 'friends' believe you are selfish and unnatural for just wanting to lead a normal life.

If you do continue the pregnancy you may find that few hospitals have staff trained in disability awareness or in signing for the deaf. Childbirth can be a frightening experience if the staff attending cannot or will not communicate accurate information and positive support. You may find it helpful to prepare a comprehensive birth plan in advance, and to find a friend or advocate to act as birth assistant, helping to communicate your needs and wishes throughout labour.

There is no evidence that parental disability is in itself harmful to children. Disabilities vary widely, of course, but there are relatively few people who cannot care adequately for a child with the benefit of practical and emotional support. As with single parenting, many of the problems faced are due to poverty, isolation and public attitudes.

Practical help
You may need to fight for additional medical help in pregnancy, practical help with childcare and sympathetic support. It is a good idea to contact one of the disability organisations or a

peer network such as the one run by the Parent Ability group of the National Childbirth Trust (see Help and Information, p. 174).

WORK

- **Is it important to you to keep working after the birth?**
- **What is important: the money, the friends, or the job itself?**
- **Can only paid employment meet these needs?**
- **Are you entitled to maternity leave?**
- **Will your employer pass you over for promotion when you are a mother?**
- **Will you be able to keep working after the birth?**
- **Can you work part-time or flexi-time or from home?**

Deciding whether to continue working once you are a mother can be hard: it may be that you are forced to, because you need the money, or it could be that, after allowing for childcare and other expenses, you will be just as well off on benefits. Whichever the case, you may want to carry on working anyway because of the friends you have there, or because you enjoy your career. It may be that you can work part-time or flexi-time for a while, if your employer is willing, or perhaps your partner can take time off. Whatever you arrange, remember not to underestimate how tired you will feel for the first few months after your child is born.

You have a statutory right not to be dismissed because you are pregnant, and to return to work after your baby is born, provided you have worked for the same employers without a break for at least 16 hours a week for two years, or at least 8 hours a week for five years by the time you are 29 weeks' pregnant. These rights may not apply if you work for a firm with five or less employees.

You have the right to time off with full pay in order to attend antenatal checkups, regardless of how long you have worked. Your employer will also be expected to make all arrangements to offer you alternative work if your usual work becomes unsuitable or hazardous because of your pregnancy. If your pregnancy makes you incapable of work, and there is no suitable alternative available, then your employer may be justified in dismissing you, but you should check this out with specialist advice.

You can return to work up to 29 weeks after the baby is born, providing that: you have worked till the end of the twelfth week before the baby is due; you have informed your employer at least 21 days before you leave that you are going on maternity leave, when the baby is due and that you intend to return; and – if your employer requests it – you can give notice in writing and enclose a copy of maternity certificate form MAT B1.

It is important to be realistic about the difficulties of combining work with childbearing: magazine features singing the praises of dynamic businesswomen who were back in the board-room six weeks after childbirth do tend to gloss over the nanny, au pair and home help hovering in the background. But don't let go of your dreams, because it *is* possible to have a great career and fantastic family. Motherhood may make it necessary to postpone or readjust your plans for a while, but not to abandon them.

Practical help
If you have been working for the same employer for 26 weeks by the 15th week before the baby is due, you can claim Statutory Maternity Pay. This is a weekly payment from your employer for 18 weeks, whether or not you intend to return to work after having the baby. SMP can be paid from the 11th week before your baby is due. To receive the full 18 weeks benefit, the latest possible start date for payment is the 6th week before the baby is due.

FINANCES

As soon as you have decided to keep your baby, you should seek advice about the financial and practical assistance available to you. There are a number of benefits you may be able to claim: start by collecting form FW8 from your doctor or midwife. Remember, if you are under 16 you are still legally a child and your parent or guardian will need to claim on your behalf.

The system of welfare benefits is very complicated, and

constantly changing. Although the information below was correct at the time of going to press, you are advised to seek specialist help. This can be from:

- **Citizens Advice Bureau (CAB)**
- **Social Security Office**
- **DSS Helpline**
- **One Parent Families**
- **Maternity Alliance**

See Help and Information, p. 174 for details.

Practical help

If you are not eligible for **Statutory Maternity Pay** (see p. 140), you are unemployed or self-employed and have paid standard rate National Insurance contributions for at least 26 weeks of the year by the time you are 26 weeks pregnant, you can claim Maternity Allowance.

If you do not qualify for **Maternity Allowance**, but have been paying NI contributions for two years, you may receive Sickness Benefit.

If you are unemployed or do not work more than 24 hours per week and are on a low income, you may get Income Support. This can also be used to top up other benefits. If you are married or have a partner only one of you can claim, and if you are under 16 you cannot claim for yourself (but your parents can claim if they are on a low income).

ALL PREGNANT WOMEN CAN CLAIM:

- **free dental treatment on the NHS while pregnant and for a year after the birth;**
- **free NHS prescriptions for you and your child while you are pregnant and for a year after the birth.**

PREGNANT WOMEN ON INCOME SUPPORT CAN ALSO CLAIM:

- free milk tokens;
- free vitamin tablets for you while pregnant and breastfeeding, and vitamin drops for your baby until the age of five;
- vouchers for glasses;
- hospital fares;
- lump sum Maternity Payment of £100.

Once the child is born every mother can claim Child Benefit. This is currently £10.40 per week for the first child. If you are in low-paid, full-time work, you may be able to claim Family Credit.

SOMEWHERE TO LIVE

- Do you have somewhere to live that is stable and comfortable?
- If not, do you plan to move?
- Who do you want to be living with?
- Do you know what facilities are available in your area for mothers?

You may have a choice between living on your own or with others – family, friends or partner. Living with other people is usually cheaper, and may give you emotional support and practical help with childcare. You do need to be sure that your flatmates or family are prepared for the disruption a new baby will cause, and that you will find their involvement helpful rather than under-mining. If you value privacy and independence, you may prefer living solo. This can work out more expensive, and you may need to make extra effort not to end up lonely or isolated.

If you are under 16 you have no right to your own home, so will usually have to stay with your family. Otherwise, you can apply for a council flat by contacting your local Housing Department.

There are often long waiting lists for council accommodation, and you may be offered bed and breakfast, or a room in a council-run hostel, or mother and baby home, instead. The anti-abortion group LIFE run a number of mother and baby homes where you will also be offered practical help and counselling. If you already have your own home but space is limited, it may be easier to rearrange the living space than to move altogether. You don't need an expensively equipped nursery for a newborn baby – most will sleep quite soundly in the same room as adults. After a few months, however, your baby may become more easily disturbed, and you may need a quietish place for it to sleep so that you don't have to tiptoe around. Your Health Visitor can advise you how to make your home safer and more suitable for a small baby.

Practical help

If you are on a low income you may be eligible for Council Tax Benefit and Housing Benefit: this will not meet heating, meals or services included in your rent. Council tenants can apply for a rent rebate, while private or housing association tenants can apply for rent allowance. If you own your own home and are on Income Support you can get help from the DSS towards the interest on your mortgage.

EDUCATION/TRAINING

- Do you want to continue with your education?
- What facilities are available in your area?
- Are you eligible for a grant?
- Do you have access to crèche or nursery facilities?

All unemployed 16- and 17-year-olds are guaranteed a place on Youth Training, but pregnant women are exempt from some schemes which are unsuitable. The trainee has the right to return to YT and finish her training up to one year after leaving to have the baby. There is no guarantee of return to the same course, and no provision of childcare allowance.

If you are still at school, then the law says you must continue with some sort of education until you reach the normal school-leaving age. The type of education you get depends not just on what you want, but also on what your local education authority has to offer. It will be one or more of the following:

Staying on at school allows you to keep up your classes and your friends. It could be your best bet if you want to do well academically. On the other hand, you could feel you don't have much in common with your classmates any more, you may be an object of curiosity, and you may feel too tired to keep up.

Home tuition may be provided for you individually or as part of a group. You may get five to ten hours a week to keep you up with the syllabus. You may find it difficult to maintain your motivation and concentration away from schoo!.

Special units combine education with facilities for young mothers. Some have a nursery on the premises. You will be taught about parenting skills together with other young women in a similar situation to yourself.

If you are over 16, you may be able to get a grant to go to college. There are a large number of courses available – both vocational and academic – and some are especially geared to the needs of working mothers or women who have been raising children. Many courses are run part-time or in the evenings, and some colleges have a nursery where your child can be cared for while you are studying.

Practical help
Advice can be obtained from the Education Welfare Officer at your local Educational Welfare Services Department, or from the Advisory Centre for Education (tel: 0181-980 4359).

CHILDCARE

- **What are the childcare facilities in your area?**
- **What kind of childcare can you afford?**
- **What will you do if your child is unhappy away from you?**
- **What will you do if your childminder falls sick?**

Childcare provision in this country is very patchy and very poor. It is a good idea to start looking around as soon as possible: you may need to get your name down on a waiting list.

Day nurseries usually take children between two and five, though a few will also take babies. They could be run by local authority, charities, or as a private business, and prices vary. Some colleges also run nurseries for their staff and students, as do some employers. Information on what is available in your area can be found at your local Social Services or Citizens Advice Bureau.

Childminders look after children in their own home. They are often flexible and can fit in with your work. Prices vary, but will almost inevitably feel very low to her and very high to you. Make sure your childminder is registered with the local Social Services Department, and visit her home before you leave your child there.

Playgroups usually run for a few hours each day, and must be registered with the Social Services. If your child is over three, you can usually leave it at the playgroup – any younger and you will usually have to stay yourself.

Parent and Toddler Groups cater for parents with younger children and babies. You must stay with your child, but it is a good way of sharing support with other mothers. They are not registered with Social Services but that department will usually hold a list of groups.

Other options include getting in a mother's help or au pair for a few hours each day, or having a live-in nanny. This is usually expensive, but can sometimes be shared with other mothers.

CHAPTER EIGHT

ADOPTION AND FOSTERING

———

If you want to continue your pregnancy, you must begin to think about your own and your baby's future. Bringing up a child on your own can be very demanding, and you may feel that you are not in a position to provide – physically and emotionally – for a child at this stage in your life. You may then want to consider adoption or fostering.

ADOPTION

Adoption is a way of providing a child with new legal parents. An adoption order cuts all legal ties with the child's family and treats the child in law as if he or she had been born into the adopted family. In other words, someone else takes full responsibility for your child, replacing you as the child's legal mother. Once the court has granted an adoption order, it is final and cannot be revoked.

FOSTERING

Fostering is a form of shared caring, which allows your child to become a temporary member of someone else's family. This arrangement can allow you weeks or months to get your situation sorted out until you are ready to provide a settled home for your baby. During that time you may visit your child on a regular basis.

MAKING YOUR DECISION

Think very carefully – this is a decision that will affect many people's lives. Get all the advice you need, and take advantage of counselling or other sources of help which are offered to you. You need to consider not just how you would cope with a baby, but how you see yourself spending the next twenty years. Remember that there are a range of options open to you: if you are ready for parenthood but experiencing difficulties right now, you may be able to get help from social services – or you might want to consider fostering until you've sorted things out.

If you are not ready for parenthood, and you cannot foresee a time in the reasonably near future when you and your baby can happily build a life together, consider adoption. This can seem a very positive alternative to abortion, and there are many couples who are very keen to adopt a baby and give it a good life.

On the other hand, you have to seriously consider whether you will feel able to hand over your baby after birth. You *can* change your mind at the last minute –many women do – but this means that you won't be practically or mentally prepared for parenthood. Once you have consented to the adoption, you cannot easily change your mind. Your child will legally belong to someone else and you may spend the rest of your life wondering – and maybe worrying – about how s/he is getting on. You will also have to explain to people where your baby has gone – and maybe carry on explaining for ever.

Studies of women who have given their children up for adoption show that this experience can cause lasting pain and loss. Women who have relinquished their children over thirty years previously report feelings of mourning, a wish to know how the child is getting on, and fear that they will never be forgiven for 'abandoning' their baby. Fortunately, most adoption agencies nowadays give natural mothers much more information and support than they did in the past.

HOW TO ARRANGE FOSTERING

If you need help with looking after your child contact the Social Services – you can get the number in the phone book or from your Citizens Advice Bureau. Explain to the social services exactly how your situation prevents you from taking your baby home straight-away, and how you could be helped to make improvements. You can ask for your child to be taken into voluntary care or 'accommodation'. The social worker may arrange for your child to be cared for in another family while you are helped with housing or money, or counselling to help you make up your mind about adoption.

You will be expected to keep up regular contact with your baby and its foster carers, so that you can develop a relationship and so lessen the shock for both of you if your baby finally comes home. The foster mother will also be a good source of support, especially if you try to see her as a friend rather than a rival: foster mothers are now trained to help you develop your own parenting skills and self-confidence.

You should also be aware, however, that the same difficulties which made you consider fostering may be seen as reasons not to return your child to you. Although social workers will normally be very helpful and concerned to reunite you with your child as soon as possible, their first duty is to the child's welfare, and if there is any reason for them to be worried that your child might be at risk in your care, you will need to convince them that you can be a 'good enough mother'. This may be particularly difficult if you are very young, or suffering from poverty. Although the social worker will often be your best ally, you should keep alert for signs of unfair prejudice or an unwillingness to listen to your wishes. If this happens, you might want to seek outside help (see Help and Information, p. 174).

HOW TO ARRANGE ADOPTION

You cannot arrange adoption yourself, unless your child is to be adopted by a close relative. All other adoptions must be arranged by an approved adoption agency, and agreed by the courts.

Your first step should be to contact your local authority's Social Services Department, whether you are considering fostering or adoption. Alternatively, you could approach a voluntary agency (see Help and Information). They will arrange for you to meet a social worker, who will ask you about your situation and your reasons for choosing adoption. They will also want to talk to the father of your child and gain his permission – though if you are unmarried, and the father does not have legal custody of your child, his permission is not obligatory and you do not have to identify him. All this information is kept confidential, and at this stage you can still change your mind. If you want to meet your baby's prospective adoptive parents, this can usually be arranged. The social worker will want to involve you in planning for the child's future, and you may want to use the opportunity to discuss your feelings about what kind of family should bring up your child.

AFTER THE BIRTH

It is a good idea to let the hospital know if your baby is to be adopted – you can then discuss with them their policy, and your wishes about how much you want to see and care for your baby until you go home. At that point, about five days after the birth, your child will either be taken by a temporary foster mother or will go straight to the adoptive parents.

When they have the baby in their care, adoptive parents will apply to the court for an adoption order. You will be visited by a 'reporting officer' who will make sure that you are giving your fully informed consent before asking you to sign your agreement. This cannot be done until your baby is at least six weeks old, so you can still change your mind.

After the baby has lived with its new parents for about three months, the social worker will check that they have all settled in happily together. The agency provides a report to the court, who will then grant an adoption order. You do not have to attend the court hearing. It is also possible to speed up this procedure by signing over your parental rights to the adoption agency when your baby is six weeks old. You may prefer this method if you have no doubts about the adoption and want to complete the procedure quickly.

CHANGING YOUR MIND

Until the time when you sign your agreement to adoption – when your child is six weeks old – you have full parental rights and responsibilities and can ask for your baby back at any time. Provided your baby is not at any risk in your care, the social services or adoption agency have to comply with your request.

After you have signed your agreement, it is not so easy to change your mind. The courts are not happy to shift children to and fro between parents, and you would need to convince them that it would be in the child's best interests to be returned to you. You would have to tell the adoption agency at once, get legal advice, and apply to the court for a review of the case.

FUTURE CONTACT WITH YOUR CHILD

If you want, you can ask for information on how your child is getting on at least until the adoption order is made, and after that if the agency and adoptive parents agree. You may even be able to arrange visits, though you will have to remember how important it is for your child and its parents that their relationship is not disrupted.

In future years, your child may be curious about you. These days, adoptive parents are encouraged to tell children from an early age that they are adopted, and to give them general information about their natural parents. You can, if you wish, write a letter for your child to read when s/he is older, telling her about yourself and your situation, and maybe including a photograph. It is best to give one copy to the adoptive parents (though it is up to them whether or not they hand it over) and another to the adoption agency or social services. You can then add to this information at any time: in future years this information may be very precious to your child.

Adopted people are often very interested in their 'roots', and they can obtain their original birth certificate – including your name – when they reach the age of 18 (17 in Scotland). They can also ask the adoption agency for information. Many will be satisfied with that information, but some may then try to trace you. Under the 1989 Children Act the Registrar General holds a 'contact register' to help with this situation, and you can tell the Registrar if you would be willing to have your child contact you. If you are not, you can have an intermediary named on the register instead so that, if your child does try to make contact, they can be told that you wish to be remain anonymous. You may also find it helpful to ask the social services or a local voluntary organization for counselling to help you sort out your feelings and wishes on this matter.

AFTER ADOPTION

People who adopt babies are usually very motivated and loving parents, who will have been assessed carefully by the adoption agency to make sure they can offer your child a good home. All families have problems, but adopted children are as likely to lead happy, stable lives as those raised in other families.

Your child will usually be raised in a family of the same ethnic origin as yourself, to help them develop understanding of and pride in their individual and social identity. If you feel strongly that you want your child to be raised in a particular culture or religion, you should discuss this with the social worker prior to adoption.

Adoption is a very difficult choice to make, and certainly not one that is popular these days. In 1970 nearly 9,000 children under one were adopted: by 1986 this figure had fallen to under 800. This is partly because it is so much easier for women to get abortions or to raise their children as single parents, partly because, in our society, it is considered somehow unnatural to separate biological from social parenthood.

Women who give up their children are sometimes considered heartless: alternatively, they may be pitied and expected to spend the rest of their lives in grief and regret. This is terribly unfair. If you decide on adoption, you are not deserting your baby, but giving it a good start in life with parents who have a lot of love to give. Because adoption is such a minority choice for women facing unwanted pregnancy, there is no shortage of families waiting to adopt babies, and you will be bringing great joy to those families.

YOUR FEELINGS AFTER ADOPTION

It is important that you take good care of yourself after the adoption, as this can be a very difficult and upsetting time. It is natural to feel sad, angry or guilty, as you have carried a baby to term and possibly felt quite a deep bond before giving your baby up. But it is also normal to feel just relieved or numb – don't think that you are unworthy or unnatural if it takes a while for deeper feelings to surface.

These feelings may be very varied: you could feel isolated and distressed, or an enormous sense of relief that the whole thing is over. If you would have kept the baby under different circumstances, your sense of loss could be very acute. If you have a partner it may be difficult for both of you to come to terms with having a child and then giving that child up, and what that means for your relationship. You may find it useful to read Chapter Six, 'After Abortion', as many of the issues detailed there may apply to your situation as well.

Other people might not help: you may have to cope with insensitive comments from people who knew you were pregnant and assumed you would be keeping the baby. They may not understand why you chose not to have an abortion, or how you could 'give your baby away'. These attitudes make it even more important that you hold onto the reasons why you chose adoption, and why it was your best option at the time. You may find it helpful to meet up with other women who have undergone a similar experience, or to seek professional counselling (see Help and Information, page 174).

Don't panic – you will not feel sad forever. You *will* remember this baby, but memories don't have to be unhappy. Grieving is a natural process, and if you look after yourself – and take all the love and support available to you – you should in time be able to live at peace with the decision you have made.

CHAPTER NINE

CONTRACEPTION

You are quite capable of becoming pregnant again immediately after abortion or childbirth, so if you don't want to become pregnant again, you will need to think about contraception. The safest way to avoid unwanted pregnancy is to avoid penetrative sex. You and your partner can make each other feel good in so many ways: kissing, touching, stroking and rubbing. Many people feel shy about this, and think it doesn't count as 'real' sex, but with trust and imagination it can be every bit as exciting and satisfying as intercourse. Most people, however, consider penetrative sex an important part of their sex lives. If this is the case, you will probably want to consider some other forms of birth control.

If you got pregnant using a particular form of contraception, then it may be quite hard for you to carry on using it after an unplanned pregnancy. You may feel suspicious that it has failed you once and will probably do so again. Pinpointing what went wrong is not always possible, but if you can, this may be reassuring: rather than blame yourself or the method you may realize what went wrong and how to avoid making the same mistake again. For instance, many women only learn through unplanned pregnancy that taking antibiotics may render the Pill ineffective. **All** methods of contraception carry some risk of failure, so an unplanned pregnancy doesn't necessarily mean that you should automatically switch to another method. The more comfortable you are with your method of contraception, the more likely you are to use it effectively.

CHOOSING YOUR METHOD OF BIRTH CONTROL

There are no 'right' and 'wrong' methods of contraception: each has its advantages and drawbacks, and it is up to you, with the help of professional advice, to assess these in the light of your individual situation.

To do this, you will need to evaluate your current situation, including:

- **your lifestyle (including number of sexual partners, frequency of intercourse, work and sleep patterns which may interfere with regular pill-taking)**
- **your age**
- **your health**
- **your need to avoid pregnancy**
- **your relationship**
- **your safer sex plan**

and also what each form of contraception can offer you:

- **failure rate (usually expressed as a percentage range, because the effectiveness will depend on how conscientiously it is used)**
- **health risks**
- **ease of use**
- **effect on your sex life**
- **acceptability to you and your partner**

The following pages will give you more details of some of the main methods of birth control. There is no one method of contraception that is best for everyone, and you may need to try out a few different methods before you find the one that suits you best. And, of course, your needs may change over time.

Very young women need to be aware that their fertility is very high, reaching its peak at age eighteen. Many doctors see sexually active teenagers as too irresponsible to use anything other than the Pill, but other methods have their own advantages. Condoms offer you some protection against sexually transmitted diseases and cervical cancer (which is a particular risk for sexually active young women).

After pregnancy you may feel sore and tired, and not much in the mood for sex anyway. Breastfeeding can in itself be a good contraceptive, but only if you are breastfeeding your baby on demand **at least** every four hours (day and night), and not supplementing its diet with formula or other feed. If you have used a diaphragm previously it will need to be refitted: condoms are fine but extra lubrication may be needed. An IUD or injectable can be used six weeks after delivery – any earlier may cause excessive bleeding. The combined pill is OK only if you are **not** breastfeeding, whereas the progestogen-only pill is also suitable for breastfeeding mothers. Natural Family Planning is fine if you are an established user, but you should not aim to start using it at this time, as your body will still be in a state of change.

Disabled women may have difficulty finding accessible family planning services and procedures, but most forms of contraception can be adapted to become suitable, with appropriate care and commitment. A blind woman may need to be shown how to orientate her packet of pills, while women with mobility problems or bad arthritis may need their partners to help them use a diaphragm or cap. It is gradually getting easier to find doctors who can give you appropriate and respectful care, and advice is also available from SPOD (see Help and Information, p. 174).

METHODS OF CONTRACEPTION

This is a rough guide only and cannot take the place of specialist medical advice. If you want more detailed information, perhaps to discuss with your partner before getting professional help, you can get free leaflets covering birth control and reproductive health from the Family Planning Association (see Help and Information, p. 174). These are available in a range of community languages.

THE PILL

The pill is an oral contraceptive which is taken by mouth, once a day. There are two main types: the 'combined' Pill, which contains the hormones oestrogen and progestogen, and the progestogen-only Pill. The combined Pill works by preventing ovulation, whereas the progestogen-only Pill thickens cervical mucus to prevent sperm from reaching the egg. The Pill is a very effective form of contraception, and side-effects can usually be cleared by switching to another brand. It must always be prescribed by a doctor – never borrow your friends' pills.
Success rate: 93–99 per cent

Advantages
The Pill is very reliable, allowing you to enjoy sex without worry or disruption. It prevents heavy periods and Premenstrual Syndrome, and can be used to prevent periods altogether. It can protect you against ovarian and uterine cancers and Pelvic Inflammatory Disease.

Disadvantages
You have to remember to take the Pill every day at a regular time. It can fail if you are on certain antibiotics, vomit, suffer very heavy diarrhoea or take it more than twelve hours late (three hours for the progestogen-only Pill). The Pill doesn't protect against HIV or STDs and may increase the risk of some infections. Side-effects can include loss of libido, weight gain, headaches, nausea, depression, sore breasts, and breakthrough bleeding (this may mean you need a different dose). Although the Pill is generally safer than you would imagine from the media scare stories, there are health risks. You should avoid the Pill if you have a history of breast cancer, liver disease, thrombosis, sickle-cell anaemia, anorexia, bulimia,

irregular periods, severe migraine, high blood-fat levels, epilepsy or a family history of strokes or heart disease at an early age. You may be advised against the Pill if you are very overweight, over 35, or a smoker, though you may still be able to use the progestogen-only Pill. This long list makes the Pill seem rather frightening. To put it in perspective, remember that non-smokers under 35 are more likely to die playing football or giving birth than from taking the Pill.

INJECTABLES (JAB, JAG, DEPO PROVERA, NORISTERAT)

This method works in a similar way to the Pill, but you do not need to remember it every day. Progestogen is injected into the muscle, and this lasts for either 8 weeks (with Noristerat) or 12 weeks (Depo Provera). It must be prescribed, and follow-up injections must be given by a doctor or nurse. Injectable methods have been controversial because of evidence that they have sometimes been given without securing fully informed consent from the clients. In particular, there are reports that it has been given, without explanation, to black, immigrant, and/or working class women, and to women after abortions. Injectables *can* be useful for some women, but as with any method, you need to understand and agree to its use.

Success rate: over 99 per cent

Advantages

Very effective, and useful for women who have difficulty remembering to take the Pill everyday. It doesn't interfere with sex, and allows you to keep contraception secret from your partner/s and parent/s. May be particularly beneficial for women suffering menstrual problems, Pelvic Inflammatory Disease, and homozygous sickle-cell disease.

Disadvantages

Side-effects include breakthrough or irregular bleeding, weight gain and depression. Long-term risks include cervical cancer and delayed fertility for up to 9 months. Injectable methods should only be offered to women who cannot find another suitable form of contraception.

THE IUD (IUCD, COIL OR LOOP)

The IUD is a small plastic device, coated with thin copper wire, that is inserted into your womb by a doctor. Thin threads are left hanging through the cervix so that you can check it is in place, and it need only be changed every five years. The IUD is thought to work in several different ways, through a combination of factors. It may stop the sperm reaching the egg to fertilize it; or it may delay the egg coming down the Fallopian tube; or it may prevent the egg from settling in the womb.
Success rate: 96–98 per cent

Advantages
The IUD is very reliable, does not interrupt sex, and works as soon as it is in place. It can be left in for years, and removed as soon as you want to conceive. You don't need to remember to use it, and need check-ups only once a year.

Disadvantages
Having the IUD fitted can be quite uncomfortable, especially if your doctor is not used to inserting them. Side-effects may include heavy bleeding, so it is best avoided if you already have difficult periods. The IUD may also exacerbate the risk of infection, so it is not suitable if you have a history of Pelvic Inflammatory Disease, HIV, other infections, or have a number of sexual partners: it is a good idea to get checked for chlamydia **before** having an IUD inserted. There is also a slightly increased risk of ectopic pregnancy, and it provides no HIV/STD protection. Your partner may feel the threads: this is not normally a problem unless the doctor has trimmed them too short, in which case they can ruck up into a bristly spike (ouch!). Occasionally, the IUD may be pushed out on its own.

THE DIAPHRAGM OR CAP

There are various styles of diaphragm or cap, all variations on a dome-shaped rubber ring which fits over your cervix. Whichever one suits you, it must be inserted together with a spermicide prior to intercourse, and then left in place for at least six hours. Diaphragms and caps need to be fitted by a doctor, and you should have it checked for size regularly and **always** after pregnancy, abortion, and weight loss or gain of 7lb/3kg or more. Never use an oil-based lubricant, as this destroys the rubber, and remember to carefully check for holes and tears before use.
Success rate: 85–96 per cent

Advantages
Diaphragms and caps are easy to use and painless. They carry no health risks, and help to protect against STDs and cervical cancer.

Disadvantages
You have to be conscientious about putting the diaphragm or cap in – not always easy if it's late, you're tired, and the thing keeps jumping out of your fingers. Insertion can be difficult, particularly if you have a disability which affects co-ordination or dexterity. You have to feel OK about putting your fingers inside your vagina, and you have to have the cap with you whenever you might want sex. If more than three hours elapse between insertion of the diaphragm or cap and sexual intercourse, more spermicide should be added. You also need to add more spermicide each time you have sex: this can get smelly and messy. Your partner may dislike the taste of spermicide (though you can get around this by using less spermicide – many women use too much anyway – by washing after insertion, or by using C-film instead of gel). Diaphragms and caps offer little or no protection against transmission of HIV. Some women find that the diaphragm (but not the cap) increases cystitis attacks: this is usually because it is the wrong size or is not being inserted properly, and can be easily remedied by a check-up at your doctor, or FPC.

THE CONDOM
(SHEATH, RUBBER, JOHNNY, FRENCH LETTER)

The condom is a thin latex sheath which is rolled over the man's erect penis just prior to intercourse. It is available from pharmacists, dispensing machines, supermarkets, garages, hairdressers or mail order – or free of charge from Family Planning Clinics.
Success rate: 85–98 per cent

Advantages
Condoms are cheap and widely available, and you don't need to visit a doctor to get them. They are easy to use, and have no health risks. You can carry them around till needed, which is useful if you have irregular sex. They provide protection against HIV, STD, infections and cervical cancer. Condoms can lessen premature ejaculation, and some men find they prolong pleasure and heighten orgasm. Many contain lubricants, which can help if you have a problem with dryness. Using a condom means your partner must share responsibility for contraception with you.

Disadvantages
Many men are reluctant to use condoms, claiming they lessen pleasure. Sometimes they burst, leak or come off. Lubricants may irritate (though non-allergenic versions are available).

THE FEMALE CONDOM

The only female condom currently available in the UK is Femidom, which is made of polyurethane. It is closed at one end, and designed to form a loose lining to the vagina with two flexible rings, one at each end, to keep it in place. Other types of female condom are expected on the market in the future. There have been no large scale studies showing how effective the female condom is, but research to date shows that it should be as effective as the male condom.

Advantages

The same advantages as the male condom, including protection against STDs, HIV, infections and cervical cancer. Useful for women whose sexual partners will not use or who have problems with male condoms. Couples may want to share responsibility by alternating between male and female condoms or they may find that the female condom suits them better than the male condom.

Disadvantages

Not suitable for women who have an infection in their vagina or cervix and some women may feel uncomfortable about inserting it. Women may find it cumbersome to use, or feel that it 'passes the buck' back to them to take responsibility for safer sex. Femidoms are more expensive than male condoms. They are available free at some but not all Family Planning Clinics.

SPERMICIDES

Spermicides contain chemicals which help destroy sperm before they can fertilize the ovum. They are easily available from clinics and pharmacists in foam, gel, pessary or cream form. There is also a product called C-film, which is like a square of cling-film impregnated with spermicide. All these are placed in the vagina just prior to intercourse. They start working within ten minutes and stay effective for up to three hours. Ideally, spermicides should be used in conjunction with a barrier method of contraception.

Success rate: Used on their own, about 75–95 per cent

Advantages

Spermicides are easy to obtain and to use, and the health risks are extremely low. Their lubricant qualities can be useful if you find dryness a problem.

Disadvantages

Spermicides are not an effective form of contraception used on their own, and you may find them disruptive as they need to be inserted less than one hour before sex, and left to melt for ten minutes (except foams which do not melt). The chemicals may irritate the delicate lining of the vagina, particularly if there is any pre-existing vaginal infection, and your partner may find the taste unpleasant. They can be messy.

NATURAL FAMILY PLANNING

Natural Family Planning involves learning about your fertility and avoiding intercourse at 'high-risk' times of the month. Your risk of getting pregnancy is highest around the time of ovulation (when the ovum is released), which normally occurs 12–16 days before the start of your next period. By identifying your fertile period, you can choose to abstain from intercourse or use an additional method of contraception at this time.

There are four main methods of NFP:

1 *Calendar method* (using the dates of your periods to work out the likely time of ovulation)
2 *Temperature method* (using a fertility thermometer to pinpoint the time of ovulation)
3 *Cervical mucus method* (monitoring changes in cervical mucus to pinpoint ovulation)
4 *Sympto-thermal method* (a combination of the above methods, together with other physical symptoms of ovulation such as position of the cervix, back or abdominal aches, breast discomfort and ovulation pain)

All of these methods rely on accurate knowledge of your own body, and will be much more effective if you are trained in their use by a qualified NFP teacher. **You are strongly advised to contact one of the specialist centres** listed in Help and Information, p. 174.
Success rate: 75–98 per cent

Advantages

NFP is very valuable for women whose religion forbids other forms of birth control. It can also be useful if you can't find a form of contraception to suit you and if pregnancy wouldn't be a total disaster. It also allows you to plan a pregnancy. There are no health risks, and the trust and intimacy required for successful NFP may enrich your sexual and emotional relationship: it is, after all, a good opportunity to experiment with other forms of sexual expression during your fertile period. NFP is very cheap, and can be tailored to suit your particular requirements. Once you have learned the technique, you don't need any professional involvement. Many couples enjoy making love without contraception.

Disadvantages

NFP can have a high failure rate if it is not used properly or if your ovulation cycle varies. It requires a great deal of commitment, shared trust and communication, and willingness to either forgo penetrative sex or to use barrier methods during the fertile period. You need to be able to keep precise records, and to watch out for anything which might disrupt your cycle, such as heavy stress or illness.

WITHDRAWAL (PULLING OUT)

Withdrawal is one of the oldest forms of birth control, and simply involves your partner making sure he ejaculates ('comes') *outside* your vagina. Although it is not usually recommended as a method of contraception, it is certainly better than no contraception at all.
Success rate: 80–95 per cent

Advantages

There are no health risks, and you may find withdrawal enhances your mutual trust and sexual creativity. Your partner has to share responsibility for birth control, and to learn that penetration need not be the focus of good sex.

Disadvantages

This method requires lots of self-control and trust, otherwise you will find it very difficult to relax and enjoy sex. Withdrawal works best with men who are comfortable with their own sexuality, and can be difficult for very young men who are still developing control over ejaculation. Most importantly, you should know that sperm pass out of the penis **before** ejaculation – about 3 million of them!

STERILIZATION AND VASECTOMY

Sterilization is an effective and permanent form of birth control. It involves a surgical operation to cut, tie or block the tubes through which the ovum travels before meeting sperm. This is an operation which often involves a stay in hospital and recuperation for a couple of days afterwards.

Men can also be sterilized: this is called vasectomy. It involves cutting, tying or blocking the tubes which feed sperm into the penis. The operation does not affect sexual performance or enjoyment, and when the man comes he will still ejaculate seminal fluid.

If you are considering sterilization as a couple, you will need to decide which of you should have the operation. Vasectomy is a safer and simpler procedure than female sterilization; but as women's fertile years end a lot sooner than men's, and circumstances change, you may feel it is a lesser risk to go for female sterilization. Whichever operation you choose, remember, **sterilization should be regarded as permanent**. It is sometimes possible to reverse the procedure, but success rates are low; so you need to be very sure that you won't regret the operation later.

Unless you have a medical reason for sterilization, you may find NHS waiting lists very long. You can pay for the operation in the non-NHS sector, either at a charity like BPAS, or in a commercial clinic. Prices start at £310 for female sterilization and £135 for vasectomy.

Many doctors are unwilling to perform sterilization if you are under 35, or do not have children. You will find the charities more flexible, though counselling will be offered to help make sure you have fully considered your choice. You do not need your partner's consent, though some doctors will prefer this. It is advised that you attend counselling as a couple.

Failure rate: Female sterilization: 1–3 per 1,000; vasectomy: 1 in 1,000.

Advantages

Sterilization is permanent and reliable. You don't need to remember it, and it doesn't affect your sex life. There are very few health risks. It is useful when you are certain that your family is complete, or that you do not want children at all, or where pregnancy would be dangerous to your health.

Disadvantages

Sterilization is usually irreversible, and requires a surgical operation. It provides no protection against HIV or other infection. In the very rare occurrence of a sterilization failure, there is a risk of ectopic pregnancy, which can be serious.

WHERE TO GO FOR CONTRACEPTIVE HELP

You are legally entitled to contraceptive advice and supplies on the NHS. This can be from a number of sources.

YOUR GP

Your family doctor can give you contraceptive advice and supplies. You can find a GP – or check that yours gives birth-control advice – by checking the lists kept in libraries, post offices, advice centres and Family Health Services Authorities. Those who give contraceptive advice have the letter 'C' after their names. This does not mean, unfortunately, that they are experienced or well trained in the full range of contraceptive methods: many have little to offer other than the Pill or IUD, and very few carry supplies of condoms.

You may prefer not to go to your own GP, though sometimes this can be an advantage as they know your medical and personal history. If you like, you are entitled to go to another family doctor for this service.

Be warned: if you are under 16 your doctor may not give you help without parental consent. S/he may respect your confidentiality, but this cannot be guaranteed.

NHS FAMILY PLANNING CLINICS

Anyone can attend a FPC if they are ordinarily resident in the UK, and lists can be found in your phone book or from an advice centre or Family Health Services Authority or from the FPA's Information Service. They have a number of advantages:

- **Your partner is welcome to accompany you.**
- **Staff are specialist, experienced and sympathetic.**
- **There will usually be a woman doctor available.**
- **Many make efforts to cater for minority ethnic communities.**
- **Other services available may include special youth information sessions, sex therapy, safer sex advice and counselling.**

Unfortunately, many clinics have been cut back in recent years, and you may have difficulty finding a clinic near to you, or which is open at convenient times. You may also worry about being seen by someone you know inside the clinic (though of course you will have seen them as well!)

BROOK ADVISORY CENTRES

Brook clinics offer family planning advice, supplies and specialist counselling to young people under 26. They are very sympathetic and helpful, and will respect your confidentiality.

Alternatively, you could go to a non-NHS service, like those run by the charities BPAS and Marie Stopes. There is usually a small charge for these services, though in some areas this will be paid by your local authority under contractual arrangements. You can find out about all clinics from the Family Planning Association (see Help and Information, p. 174).

SAFER SEX

As well as protecting yourself against unwanted pregnancy, you will need to think about safer sex. This will help protect you against HIV, sexually transmitted diseases (STDs), chlamydia, cervical cancer, and infections such as thrush and cystitis. Each individual has to make their own choice to what extent to practise safer sex; you may want to discuss it with your partner or any potential partners. It is important to bear in mind, though, that you cannot tell if someone has the HIV virus (or any other STD for that matter); your partner will probably have had sexual relationships in the past even if s/he is faithful to you now.

Practising safer sex is a sensible way of protecting yourself. It means you do not have to rely on the other person being honest about their sexual history, nor do you have to assume that they have not got the virus when they may have been at risk. It is a bit like wearing a seat belt when you drive a car: if you don't, it does not mean you are going to have a crash, but if you do, it may well save your life.

The three body fluids which contain enough of the HIV virus to infect you are blood, semen and vaginal fluid. In order to contract HIV you have to get a visible amount of one of these fluids directly into the bloodstream. This is not an easy process and there is no risk of HIV infection through casual contact. There are a lot of things you can do sexually which will not put you at risk. Unprotected anal or vaginal sex are the most likely ways the virus can be passed. A condom will protect you adequately unless it breaks or comes off. If you do have an accident with a condom it does not mean you will automatically get the virus if your partner is infected.

Contraception

GOOD CONDOM USE

Condoms can fail when they are not used properly. If you got pregnancy because of an accident with a condom you may be reluctant to carry on using them in the future. If it is very important for you to avoid pregnancy or you have doubts about condoms, try doubling up – either by using two barrier methods, the cap and the sheath together, or by taking the Pill and also using condoms. Although this may seem like hard work it may be worth it for peace of mind.

In addition, here are some tips and information about using condoms:

- Always use British Standard kitemarked condoms (Durex and Mates are two of the most popular brands) and check the sell-by date.
- Make sure they don't get damaged by sharp objects like keys or jewellery when they are being carried around.
- Never use massage oil, vaseline or any other oil-based lubricant with a condom as it rots the rubber. K-Y Jelly (a water-based lubricant) is fine.
- If you have problems with condoms breaking or you want to have anal sex, use the stronger ones on the market, with plenty of K-Y Jelly. Don't use two condoms together, they cause friction and split.
- Make sure your partner's penis is erect when you put the condom on. Hold the teat between your thumb and forefinger to expel the air (air trapped inside the condom is one of the reasons why they split). Be careful of tearing the condom on fingernails and rings when you put it on.
- If your partner is unsure of or embarrassed by condoms, suggest he practises putting them on and masturbating with one on when he is alone. He may feel he can get used to them better this way.
- Make sure your partner withdraws before he completely loses his erection. This way the condom is less likely to come off inside you.

169

- Have fun! There are ribbed and coloured condoms on the market. Try to incorporate them into your sex life in a positive way. It can be very erotic for you to put a condom on your partner. Using a condom may postpone his orgasm which could be pleasurable for both of you.

OTHER THINGS YOU CAN DO

There are plenty of ways to have sexual pleasure and bring each other to orgasm without intercourse. Because HIV is only present in saliva in tiny amounts (you would have to get two bucketfuls into your bloodstream at one go to be at risk) kissing is safe. Massaging each other, masturbating each other – touching or coming on the outside of the body – are also safe. Sex toys are safe providing they are not shared. Fantasy is safe providing you enjoy it.

Oral sex is also relatively safe. There may be a small possibility of contracting the virus through oral sex if you get pre-come or come in your mouth and it finds its way into your bloodstream. This risk will increase if you have cuts or sores in your mouth or damage in the lining of your throat. Oral sex is a lot less risky than intercourse, but if you are worried you can buy flavoured condoms. Your partner can give you oral sex through a cut-up condom or a dental dam (these are thin latex sheets you can buy from some dental suppliers).

The exciting thing about safer sex is that it invites you to use your imagination. It may mean that you end up with a much more interesting sex life.

LIVING WITH YOUR DECISION

—

Life goes on – sometimes all too quickly – and before you know it your unplanned pregnancy will be in the past. By taking active control of your pregnancy and choosing how best to resolve it, you have made a very powerful statement about your ability to take control of your own life. This should help you to move forward with increased maturity and confidence.

Facing unwanted pregnancy is, for many women, the first time that they have fully appreciated the implications of their fertility. If you chose abortion or adoption, you may find yourself feeling very drawn to babies and children afterwards: some women start a new pregnancy and bear a child very soon after abortion. This does not in itself mean that abortion was the wrong decision: it can act as a catalyst to deciding what you want from life and arranging your situation and relationships accordingly.

For many other women, getting pregnant forces them to face up to just how big a step it is to become a parent. When they later bear children at a more suitable time in their lives, they may be amazed at how they could have even considered coping with a baby before.

There are others to whom the experience of unplanned pregnancy brings home the realization that they do not want children at all, but have other plans for their lives. Our society still expects women to become mothers, and it can be quite difficult to stick up for what you want in the face of pressure from friends, parents and partners. Remember, it is better by far to realize you do not want children *before* the event!

Another possibility you may have to face is that childlessness will be forced upon you, because you do not ever find yourself in the right situation to bring up a child, or because of illness or infertility (the fact that you have 'proved' your fertility once does not guarantee that you or your partner will not have problems with pregnancy in the future). Up to 1 in 6 couples have difficulty conceiving a baby of their own: faced with the upset of repeated miscarriage or subfertility you may be tempted to blame yourself for an earlier abortion. It is, in fact, extremely rare for abortion to cause later fertility problems, but you should seek help for these feelings, rather than suppressing them in a welter of guilt.

If you have chosen to continue your pregnancy and keep the baby, you will be living with your decision for a very long time to come. Nevertheless, you will learn from your unplanned pregnancy in ways that may be similar to women who have opted to postpone or avoid motherhood. As your relationship with your child develops and changes, so too will your opportunities and freedoms. It can be easy – especially in the bewildering exhaustion of early motherhood – to see childrearing as directly contradictory to having a career, or continuing your education, or travelling the world. But the skills and experiences of parenthood will build on the thinking and soul-searching you have put in to get you through this pregnancy: you may become more aware of what you want from life, and more committed to achieving it.

However you have chosen to deal with your unplanned pregnancy, it can be worthwhile reminding yourself what this experience has taught you about your own feelings about the place of parenting in your life – *not* because you need to justify your decision to anyone else, but to enlarge your own understanding. Whatever choice you have made, and whatever the reasons for that choice, hold on to the knowledge that your decision was probably the most responsible and caring one open to you at the time. Adult life is all about taking responsibility for our actions and making the best we can of them, for good or ill. If you have chosen with care and wisdom, and been supported by those around you, you should find that there is no need to continue punishing yourself.

If you find that you cannot move on from unplanned pregnancy into the future, because distress and confusion are keeping you rooted in the past, don't be afraid to seek specialist help. More and more people are choosing counselling to help them get through other life crises such as divorce and bereavement – and you should not be afraid or ashamed to use the resources listed under Help and Information, p. 174, in whatever way suits you best.

Unplanned pregnancy is a crisis: but it doesn't have to be a tragedy. Use the knowledge and skills you have learned through this time, and apply them to making whatever future you have chosen as fulfilled and as positive as you can.

HELP AND INFORMATION

COUNSELLING AND ADVISORY SERVICES

Asian Women's Resource Centre, 134 Minet Ave., London NW10 8AP. Tel: 0181-961 5701.

British Association for Counselling, 1 Regent Place, Rugby CV21 2PJ. Tel: 01788-578328. BAC can suggest counsellors in your area and suitable for your situation.

Relate (formerly Marriage Guidance Council), Herbert Gray College, Little Church Street, Rugby, Warwickshire CV21 3AP. Tel: 01788-573241. Relationship counselling – you don't have to be married – ring for local number.

Samaritans, 10 The Grove, Slough, Berks SL1 1QP. Tel: 01753-532713. National network of telephone befriending for the suicidal and despairing – see your local phone book for details.

Rape Crisis, LRCC, PO Box 69, London WC1X 9NJ. National network of telephone counselling lines for women and girls who have been raped or sexually assaulted. Branches nationwide, including London: 0171-837 1600; Birmingham: 0121-766 5366; Manchester: 0161-834 8784; Edinburgh: 0131-556 9437.

Citizens Advice Bureaux can provide free advice and information on almost any problem you're likely to face. Look in the local telephone directory for your nearest branch.

National Drug Helpline Tel: 0800 776600.

Standing Conference on Drug Abuse (SCODA), Waterbridge House, 32–36 Lomon Street, London SE1 0EE. Tel: 0171-928 9500. Information on where to find personal advice and counselling for problems related to drug abuse.

London Black Womens Health Action Project, Cornwall Avenue Community Centre, 1 Cornwall Ave., London E2 0HW. Tel: 0181-980 3503. Advice, counselling, information and educational material.

London Lesbian and Gay Switchboard, BM Switchboard, London WC1N 3XX. Tel: 0171-837 7324. Free 24-hour confidential advice, counselling and referral for women who are, or think they might be, lesbian. There are many local L and G switchboards and Lesbian Lines – look in your telephone directory for details.

Shelter (National Campaign for the Homeless). Head Office: 88 Old Street, London EC1V 9HU. Tel: 0171-253 0202. Emergency Nightline: 0800 446441. Advice and information on homelessness and housing problems.

NAFSIYAT (Inter-cultural therapy centre), 278 Seven Sisters Road, London N4 2HY. Tel: 0171-263 4130 (24-hour answering service). Offers specialized therapeutic help to people from ethnic and cultural minorities.

Womens Aid Federation, PO Box 391, Bristol BS99 9WS. Over 120 refuges nationwide for women threatened by mental, emotional or physical violence or abuse. General information: 01179-633494; London helpline: 0171-251 6537; Manchester helpline: 0161-839 8574.

Womens Therapy Centre, 6 Manor Gardens, London N7. Tel: 0171-263 6200.

Womens Health, 52–54 Featherstone Street, London EC1 8RT. Tel: 0171-251 6580. Information on all aspects of women's health.

Youth Access Magazine, Business Centre, 11 Newark Street, Leicester LE1 5SS. Tel: 01509-210420. Can refer you to an appropriate young people's advisory service in your area.

ABORTION
CHARITY ABORTION SERVICES

British Pregnancy Advisory Service (BPAS) is a national charity offering abortion advice and help, pregnancy testing, contraceptive advice, emergency contraception, cervical smears, sterilization and post-abortion counselling. It has twenty-six branches and seven clinics across the country including London 0171-637 8962 or 0171-828 2484; Birmingham 0121-643 1461; Glasgow 0141-204 1832; Liverpool 0151-709 1558.

For full details of local branches, contact Head Office, Austy Manor, Wootton Wawen, Solihull, West Midlands B95 6BX. Tel: 01564-793225.

Marie Stopes Clinic is a charity offering abortion advice and help, contraceptive advice, pregnancy testing, at the following branches: **Marie Stopes House,** 108 Whitfield Street, London W1P 5BE. Tel: 0171-388 0662; **Marie Stopes Centre,** 10 Queens Square, Leeds LS2 8AG. Tel: 0113-240685; **Marie Stopes Centre,** 1 Police Street, Manchester M2 7LQ. Tel: 0161-832 4260.

There are also a number of commercial clinics offering abortion advice and help at competitive rates: details are available in your phone book or from your CHC/CAB.

ABORTION INFORMATION AND SUPPORT

Contact Charity Abortion Services for information on post abortion counselling.

Brook Advisory Centres (*see under* Contraception).

Post-Abortion Counselling Service, 340 Westbourne Park Road, W11 1EQ. Tel: 0171-221 9631. Group and individual counselling. Fees on a sliding scale for up to ten sessions.

FOETAL ABNORMALITY

Support After Termination for Foetal Abnormality (SATFA)
73–75 Charlotte Street, London W1P 1LB. Helpline No.
0171-631 0285. Admin: 0171-631 0280. Support and advice
for those who are facing, or who have had, abortion because of
foetal abnormality.

Contact-A-Family, 170 Tottenham Court Road, London W1P
0HA. Tel: 0171-383 3555. National charity for families with
children with special needs and disabilities. Network of over
700 parent-support groups, quarterly newsletter, fact sheets,
professional advice.

IRISH WOMEN

* indicates post-abortion counselling is available.

*** Ulster Pregnancy Advisory Association,** 719a Lisburn Road,
Belfast 9. Tel: Belfast 381345. Pregnancy counselling and
information on abortion services in England.

*** Dublin Well Woman Centre,** 73 Lower Leeson Street, Dublin
2. Tel: Dublin 610083. Counselling, advice, information,
contraceptive services, pregnancy testing. DWWC is not
allowed to give information on abortion services in England.

*** Irish Womens Abortion Support Group (IWASG),** c/o
Womens Health, 52–54 Featherstone Street, London EC1
8RT. Tel: 0171-251 6580. Practical and emotional support for
women coming to England for abortion.

*** Liverpool Abortion Support Service** and **Escort** can be
contacted via Liverpool BPAS.

*** Irish Family Planning Association,** 36–37 Lower Ormond
Quay, Dublin 1. Tel: Dublin 8725033.

Northern Ireland Family Planning Association, 113
University Street, Belfast BT7 1HP. Tel: Belfast 325488.

Barnardo's Adoption Counselling Service, Tel: Dublin 453
0355.

CHERISH (Organisation For One Parent Families), 2 Lower

Pembroke St., Dublin 2. Tel: Dublin 668 2744.
Rape Crisis Centre, 70 Lower Leeson Street, Dublin 2. Tel:
Dublin 661 4911. Freephone: 1800 778888.
National Pregnancy Helpline (Run by Irish FPA): 1850
495051.

CONTRACEPTION

Brook Advisory Centres provide pregnancy testing, counselling,
contraceptive advice and abortion referral for young women.
Branches nationwide – Head Office: 165 Grays Inn Road,
London WC1X 8UD. For information and advice ring Brook
Advisory Helpline on 0171-713 9000.
Family Planning Association, 27–35 Mortimer Street, London
W1N 7RJ. Tel: 0171-636 7866/631 0555. Information by
telephone (9–5 Mon.–Thurs., 9–4.30 Fri.) or letter on contra-
ception, family planning and health. Can give you the address of
your nearest family planning clinic. Leaflets and books available.
Natural Family Planning Centre, Birmingham Maternity
Hospital, Queen Elizabeth Medical Centre, Edgbaston,
Birmingham B15 2TG. Tel: 0121-472 1377, ext. 4219.

SEXUAL HEALTH

National AIDS Helpline. Tel: 0800 567123. Free and confiden-
tial 24-hour helpline for those concerned about HIV/ AIDS.
There are additional freefone lines available in the following
languages:
Cantonese, Mandarin, 6–10 p.m., Tuesday. Tel: 0800 282446;
Punjabi, Bengali, Hindi, Urdu, Gujarati, 6–10 p.m.,
Wednesday. Tel: 0800 282445;
Arabic, 6–10 p.m., Wednesday. Tel: 0800 282447;
Minicom for deaf/hard of hearing, 10 a.m.–10 p.m. every day.
Tel: 0800 521361.
Ring 0800 555777 (24-hour) for health literature.

Help and Information

Positively Women, 5 Sebastian Street, London EC1V 0HE. Admin tel: 0171-490 5501; Client services tel: 0171-490 5515, 10 a.m.–4 p.m., Monday–Friday. Counselling, information and support by and for women who are HIV positive or who have AIDS.

The Association to Aid the Sexual and Personal Relationships of People with a Disability (SPOD), 286 Camden Road, London N7 0BJ. Tel: 0171-607 8851.

CHOOSING MOTHERHOOD

Gingerbread, 35 Wellington Street, London WC2B 5AU. Tel: 0171-240 0953. Nationwide network of self-help groups for one-parent families.

Lifeline, 1st Floor, Ruskin Building, 191 Corporation Street, Birmingham. Tel: 0121-233 1641. Advice, counselling and support for women wishing to continue their pregnancy. Mother and baby home.

LIFE, LIFE House, 1a Newbold Terrace, Leamington Spa, Warwickshire CV32 4EA. Tel: 01926-421587/311667, and National Hotline, Tel: 01926-311511. LIFE is an anti-abortion organization which offers free pregnancy testing and practical help with continuing the pregnancy.

National Council for One Parent Families, 255 Kentish Town Road, London NW5 2LX. Tel: 0171-267 1361. Free information and advice on housing, welfare benefits, maintenance, legal rights and divorce for lone parents.

Youth Support, 13 Crescent Road, London BR3 2NF. Tel: 0181-650 6296 or 0181-659 9926. Residential care, counselling, childcare, training and advice for teenage mothers.

Rainer Foundation, 89 Blackheath Hill, London SE10 8TJ. Tel: 0181-694 9497. Charity for young people aged 13–21, especially young mothers. 'Handbook for Young Mothers' and 'Benefits Information Pack' free to young people.

Maternity Alliance, 15 Britannia Street, London WC1X 9JN. Tel: 0171-837 1265. Campaigns for improvements in mater-

179

nity services and provides information about rights and services for mothers, fathers and babies. Free leaflets include 'Money for mothers and babies' and 'Pregnant at Work' (send SAE).

Department of Social Security (DSS), Freefone, Tel: 0800-666555. Confidential advice given on welfare benefits.

National Childbirth Trust, Alexandra House, Oldham Terrace, London W3 6NH. Tel: 0181-992 8637. NCT aims to help women have their babies happily and without fear, and to prepare young families for the experience of childbirth and parenthood. Local branches run antenatal classes, postnatal support groups and offer free information and counselling on breastfeeding. Some branches also have specialist support groups, e.g., miscarriage, Caesarian, working mothers.

National Childcare Campaign (Day Care Trust), The Wheel, 4 Wild Court, London WC2B 5AU. Tel: 0171-405 5617. Information, support and advice about nursery provision and other childcare facilities for parents, employers and providers.

One Parent Families Scotland, 13 Gayfield Square, Edinburgh EH1 3NX. Tel: 0131-556 3899. Advice and information for single parents.

One Plus: One Parent Families Strathclyde, 55 Renfrew Street, Glasgow G2 6BD. Tel: 0141-333 1450. Advice and information for single parents in Strathclyde.

ADOPTION AND FOSTERING

British Agencies for Adoption and Fostering (BAAF), Skyline House, 200 Union Street, London SE1 0LX. Tel: 0171-593 2000. BAAF produces books and leaflets about all aspects of adoption and can put you in touch with adoption agencies in your area.

National Foster Care Association (NFCA), Leonard House, 5–7 Marshalsea Road, London SE1 1EP. Tel: 0171-828 6266. Information and leaflets about all aspects of foster care.

Post Adoption Centre, Interchange Building, 15 Wilkin Street, London NW5 3NG. Tel: 0171-284 0555.

INDEX

Of further interest . . .

The Manual of
NATURAL FAMILY PLANNING

New Edition

Dr Anna M. Flynn & Melissa Brooks

During her hormonal cycle, a woman's body shows various signs and symptoms of fertility that can be recognised and interpreted. Once learnt, fertility awareness can be used with accuracy to work out when a woman is most fertile, and an informed choice can be made about avoiding or planning a possible pregnancy.

Natural family planning is becoming increasingly popular as women move away from invasive drugs and devices and take back control of their bodies and their fertility.

This new edition is fully updated to contain all recent developments in fertility research and includes a new chapter discussing the most advanced techniques available for assessing fertile and non-fertile phases in the cycle.

Recommended by the Family Planning Association

WHY THEY CRY

Understanding Child Development
in the First Year

Hetty Van de Rijt & Frans Plooij

"Some days when I'm at a low ebb, I wonder if I'm doing the right thing, especially when I have to cope with his constant crying. I'm not always sure whether I should let him cry or pick him up and give him a cuddle.'

Every parent will identify with this statement at some point in their baby's first year. Almost all babies go through disturbing periods. In *Why They Cry* you will find positive advice to help you and your baby through the difficult times and on to each new exciting stage of development.

With this book you will learn:

- which special signs tell you your baby is about to take a major leap forward in development
- how to choose the right games and toys for each new stage
- to recognize and applaud your baby's attempts to exercise new skills
- how to chart your baby's own unique development in the first year of life.

Most of all, you will gain peace of mind and confidence in your own ability to bring up your baby.

EASY PREGNANCY WITH YOGA

The Gentle and Effective Way to
Pre- and Post-Natal Health

Stella Weller

Easy Pregnancy with Yoga is a practical workbook offering a safe, natural programme of exercise and relaxation to help you enjoy a healthy pregnancy and a confident delivery.

With the help of sixty clear black and white drawings you will learn:

- breathing and relaxation exercises
- safe, simple, controlled stretching exercises done with concentration and synchronized breathing
- to sit, stand, bend, get up and lie down without harming yourself or incurring pain
- stress management techniques which are easy to incorporate into busy daily schedules.

The book also offers helpful advice on nutrition and diet, caesarean birth and how to regain muscle tone and function after birth.

Easy Pregnancy With Yoga is essential reading not only for expectant mothers, but also for their partners and health educators.

GIRL OR BOY?

Your Chance to Choose

Hazel Phillips with Tessa Hilton

What determines the sex of your child? Can it be related to health? Diet? Ovulation cycles? Is it to do with science? Genetics? Luck? Or is it just a question of timing?

Hazel Phillips had two daughters and was very keen that her third child should be a son. With thought and careful planning she devised a safe, simple – and successful – formula to get the mixed family she wanted. She has since had testimonies from many other families to say that her method has worked for them too.

Now this fascinating and practical book explains her theories expressing in simple terms the biology of conception, tests for determining the sex of your child and factors that determines sex, to make her method available to everyone.

BORN TOO EARLY

A Practical Guide for Parents of Babies Born Prematurely

Pete Moore

For parents and the immediate family, the birth of any baby is an emotional time, but when a baby is born up to three months early it may be traumatic. Medical advances in recent years mean that many of these tiny babies will survive, but only after weeks of intensive hospital care.

Born Too Early is written in association with Action Research, a leading UK charity renowned for its vital contribution in the field of birth prematurity. Produced with the help of many experts, this book is a comprehensive guide to the medical care that premature babies receive while they are in a neonatal baby unit. Without using technical jargon, it clearly explains many of the procedures that these babies face and the equipment used to monitor their progress.

Whilst it can be difficult for parents to feel comfortable in a neonatal unit, their presence and the contribution they make is vital. With the information and advice in *Born Too Early* parents should feel reassured and more able to play their role in partnership with medical and nursing staff, ensuring that their baby has the best possible chance for a healthy future.

WATER BIRTH

The Concise Guide to Using Water During Pregnancy, Birth and Infancy

Janet Balaskas & Yehudi Gordon

Water Birth is written for expectant parents and their birth attendants. It is the first book to give comprehensive and practical information on the use of water throughout pregnancy, birth and during infancy.

Modern maternity practices are changing. Today more women are seeking to avoid the routine 'high tech' approach and are choosing to give birth using natural and active methods. For many, this means deliberately choosing to labour and give birth in or near to water.

Introducing a deep pool of warm water to the birthing room is a way to make labour shorter, easier and more comfortable. It increases the mother's sense of privacy and makes the baby's entry into the world gentle and free from trauma, whether the birth occurs in or beside the pool.

Water Birth is straightforward and detailed, reassuring and supportive. A companion volume to *New Active Birth*, it provides encouragement and all the necessary advice for parents contemplating a waterbirth and the midwives who will attend them in labour.